C000245364

Liturgical Orientation: the Position of the President at the Eucharist

Neil Xavier O'Donoghue

*Priest of the Roman Catholic Church, Vice Rector of Redemptoris Mater
Archdiocesan Missionary Seminary, Dundalk, Co. Louth, Ireland*

Subscriptions

(for two copies): individual rate £15; international (includes airmail) £22.
Single copies cost £7.99

Cheques should be made payable to Hymns Ancient & Modern Ltd , and sent
to: JLS Subscriptions, Subscription Manager, 13a Hellesdon Park Road,
Norwich NR6 5DR.

Tel: 01603 785 910   Fax: 01603 624483.
JLS@hymnsam.co.uk

Direct Debit forms available from the same address or visit
www. jointliturgicalstudies.hymnsam.co.uk

The cover image shows Fr Franz Wasner celebrating the mass for the Von Trapp family,
used by permission of Johannes Von Trapp.

ISSN: 0951-2667
ISBN: 978-1-84825-960-7

Contents

Introduction

When future histories of Christianity will deal with the twentieth century, they will undoubtedly pay a lot of attention to the changes in worship and liturgical practice that occurred across denominational lines in the decades following the second Vatican Council. Even if this Council was strictly a Roman Catholic affair, in particular, the effects of the liturgical renewal it promoted in the Church of Rome were to overflow into most areas of world Christianity in a type of liturgical cross-fertilization.[1]

As the twentieth century Orthodox liturgical experience shows us, it would be a mistake strictly to equate liturgical change and renewal with limited changes in ritual books. White's history of Roman Catholic liturgy dealing with the period when there was an almost monolithic collection of ritual texts has disproven the 'myth ... that very little happened between the end of the Council of Trent on December 4, 1563, and Vatican II'.[2] Although the Roman Catholic church has published new ritual editions for all of her liturgies over the course of the last few decades, it could also be said that perhaps these were not the most profound liturgical changes within twentieth century Roman Catholicism.

Today most liturgical scholars would agree with Cardinal Ratzinger when he lists the turning of the altars and the introduction of *versus populum* ('facing the people') celebration of the mass as being one of the most obvious and universal effects of liturgical renewal in the

---

[1] Even those churches of eastern liturgical heritage, which did not renew their liturgical rites *per se*, were also strongly influenced by the liturgical movement. See Nicholas Denysenko, *Liturgical Reform After Vatican II: the Impact on Eastern Orthodoxy* (Fortress Press, Minneapolis, MN, 2015)

[2] James White, *Roman Catholic Worship: Trent to Today* (Liturgical Press, Collegeville, MN, 2003), xiii.

wake of Vatican II.[3] In the last fifty years *versus populum* celebrations of the eucharist have become virtually universal in the Roman Catholic Church. The practice has also become an example of liturgical cross-fertilization and has passed over into the worship practices of most protestant churches that regularly celebrate the eucharist.

However, half a century after the widespread adoption of *versus populum* celebration of the eucharist, there continues to be some debate as to its advisability. In recent years some scholars and other opinion-makers have been calling on worshipping communities to reject *versus populum* celebration and exclusively celebrate mass *ad orientem* (facing east, which usually means that the priest celebrates the eucharist with his back to the assembly). Certain blogs celebrate whenever news is broadcast of some bishop or priest adopting *ad orientem* worship in any corner of the globe, seeing it as a 'brick by brick' rolling back of a liturgical dumbing down that they perceive in the wake of the second Vatican Council that was foisted on the people of God under false pretences and labelled as reform of the liturgy. Some view this change as having contributed to a loss of the sense of the sacred in liturgy. This has led to an unfortunately polemical view on this matter and the direction the celebrant faces during the eucharistic prayer has become a rallying call on both sides of the liturgical divide.

This liturgical debate became particularly heated in the summer of 2016 when Cardinal Robert Sarah, the prefect of the Congregation for

---

[3]Joseph Ratzinger, *Theology of the Liturgy: The Sacramental Foundation of Christian Existence.* Volume 11 of his (Michael J.Miller, ed) *Collected Works* (Ignatius Press, San Francisco, 2014), 393. The widespread adoption of the vernacular in the liturgy is the other major post-conciliar renewal within Roman cathoicism. See my 'Words of Salvation: the Vernacular in Contemporary Catholic Liturgy' in Thomas R. Whelan and Liam M. Tracey (eds), *Serving Liturgical Renewal: Pastoral and Theological Questions. Essays in Honour of Patrick Jones* (Veritas, Dublin, 2015), 55-69. Frequent communion is the third game-changing liturgical innovation of twentieth century catholicism, even though this renewal took place under St Pius X at the start of the twentieth century and predated the second Vatican Council by more than half a century. See Joseph Dougherty, *From Altar-Throne to Table: The Campaign for Frequent Holy Communion in the Catholic Church* (Scarecrow Press, Lanham, MD, 2010).

Divine Worship, publicly called on Roman Catholic priests to adopt the *ad orientem* posture as their normal orientation when praying the eucharistic prayer. The cardinal proposed the first Sunday of Advent of 2016 as a date to adopt this practice. As will be seen below, this proposal was not widely adopted. However, while *versus populum* has remained as the default orientation for Roman Catholics, it has been noted during the recent controversy that surprisingly little has been written on this important aspect of contemporary liturgy. Therefore this study aims at providing a brief historical background to the practice. While the treatment of liturgical orientation is from an explicitly Roman Catholic perspective, it is hoped that the history can help the shared reflection of the different churches and liturgical assemblies. This is a particular duty of those who play any part in leading the worship in every Christian liturgical assembly, as they are morally obliged to reflect pastorally on what is the best liturgical practice for their own assembly and how best to help their assembly draw nearer to Christ. This study can only provide some rather broad brushstrokes on the issues involved and hopefully these will help inspire more rigorous reflection on these issues.[4]

---

[4]In this treatment the eastern rites and various practices of the Orthodox Churches are not considered, as these churches have not seen any widespread promotion of the *versus populum* orientation. However, while not as pressing an issue, this debate is not unknown in contemporary Orthodoxy; see Robert Taft, 'Between Progress and Nostalgia: Liturgical Reform and the Western Romance with the Christian East; Strategies and Realities' in Christian McConnell (ed), *A Living Tradition: On the Intersection of Liturgical History and Pastoral Practice* (Liturgical Press, Collegeville, MN, 2012), 20-21.

1

Historical Background: the Early Church

The Christian altar has evolved from the table (or tables) used by Jesus in the Last Supper. Gathering for the 'breaking of the bread' was one of the most important activities of the first Christians.[5] Unfortunately there are no archaeological remains of the earliest Christian altars.[6] To be honest, we do not know much about the specific details of the earliest Christian eucharistic celebrations.[7] In our particular case, when dealing

---

[5]See Acts 2.42, 46; 20.7, 11 and the many other scriptural references provided in *Catechism of the Catholic Church* 335. For more on the cultural background of the Last Supper (referring to both Jewish and Hellenic meal traditions), see Dennis E. Smith, *From Symposium to Eucharist: The Banquet in the Early Christian World* (Fortress Press, Minneapolis, MN, 2003).

[6]The definitive study on the Christian altar is Joseph Braun, *Der Christliche Altar in Seiner Geschichtlichen Entwicklung*. Vol. 1: *Arten, Bestandteile, Altargrab, Weihe, Symbolik* and Vol. 2: *Die Ausstattung des Altars, Antependien, Velen, Leuchterbank, Stufen, Ciborium und Baldachin, Retabel, Reliquien- und Sakramentsaltar, Altarschranken* (Alte Meister Guenther Koch & Co, Munich, 1924). Other general historical treatments can be found in Cyril E. Pocknee, *The Christian Altar in History and Today* (Mowbray, London, 1963) and in José Antonio Iñiguez Herrero, *El Altar Cristiano*. Vol. 1: *De los Origines a Carlomagno* and Vol. 2: *De Carlomagno al Siglo XIII* (Eunsa, Pamplona, 1978, 1991 – the author died before he could complete the projected series). For a more recent summary of current scholarship see Éric Palazzo, *L'Espace Rituel et le Sacré dans le Christianisme: La Liturgie de l'Autel Portative dans l'Antiquité et au Moyen Âge* (Brepols, Turnhout, 2008), 1-4; and Heid provides a well-researched and thought-provoking re-reading of the traditional history, see Stefan Heid, 'The Early Christian Altar–Lessons for Today' in Alcuin Reid (ed), *Sacred Liturgy: The Source and Summit of the Life and Mission of the Church* (Ignatius Press, San Francisco, 2014), 87-114.

[7]For example in the famous Dura-Europos House Church, the earliest extant Christian place of worship, archaeologists did not find a prominent altar and are even unsure where exactly it was located. In contrast the baptistery is very developed (see Paul Post, 'Dura Europos Revisited: Rediscovering Sacred Space' in *Worship* 86 (2012), 222–44). This is not to say that we know nothing of the early eucharist. Many authors have treated this topic; for my own thoughts on the subject see Neil Xavier O'Donoghue, 'The Shape of the History of the Eucharist' in *New Blackfriars*

with the issue of the direction faced by the celebrant as he prayed the eucharistic prayer, we simply do not know in what direction the celebrant faced during the first few centuries of the Christian era. It is possible that there was a general common practice regarding the direction in which he faced, but it is also quite likely that there was none and each celebrant faced in whatever direction he found to be most convenient or whatever made most sense, given the place in which he was celebrating and the size and location of his assembly. When considering the early historical material, we ought to bear in mind that concerns that seem very important today are not necessarily the same concerns as Christians had almost two thousand years ago.

There is some evidence of the first Christians using portable altars before the Peace of Constantine. These were gradually replaced with permanent stone altars soon after the legalization of Christianity in the fourth century, although wooden altars were still to be found in Charlemagne's domain in the ninth century and in Ireland until the late twelfth century.[8] The size and form of the altar was also influenced by the cult of the martyrs. The earlier romantic idea of Christians gathering to celebrate in the catacombs cannot be sustained in the light of modern scholarship.[9] However the eucharist was celebrated on the tombs of the martyrs on the anniversary of their death. When Christians were allowed to build their own permanent churches, the bodies of the martyrs were often transferred into these new churches, and the style of the earlier stone tombs of the martyrs may have contributed to the popularity of

---

93 (2012), 71-83. However for another reading of the evidence of Dura Europos cf. M. J. Moreton, 'Eis anatolas blepsete: Orientation as a Liturgical Principle' in E. A. Livingstone (ed), *Studia Patristica: Papers Presented at the Ninth International Conference on Patristic Studies held in Oxford 1983*: Vol. 18.2 (Peeters, Leuven, 1989), 577-578.

[8]Neil Xavier O'Donoghue, *The Eucharist in Pre-Norman Ireland* (Notre Dame University Press, Notre Dame, IN, 2011), 165.

[9]Richard Krautheimer with Slobodan Curcic, *Early Christian and Byzantine Architecture* (4th edn, Yale University Press, New Haven, CT, 1986), 30.

the use of stone in the construction of altars.[10] As Christianity soon became the dominant religion in the Empire, there was a gradual re-dedication of some pagan temples as Christian churches. In certain cases pagan altars were even repurposed as Christian altars. In the early fifth century, for example, St Peter Chrysologus tells how '[pagan] shrines are changed into churches, pagan altars are turned into Christian altars.'[11] The reuse of pagan altars, or at least a tendency to imitate them, may be yet another reason for the widespread adoption of stone as the normal building material for altars.

During late antiquity the altar itself was the primary symbol or locus of the presence of Christ in the church building.[12] As St Ambrose said, 'what is Christ's altar unless the image of Christ's body?'[13] When St Monica is dying, she tells her sons: 'Lay this body wherever it may be. Let no care of it disturb you. This only thing I ask of you: that you should remember me at the altar of the Lord wherever you may be.'[14] This is well before there was any thought of St Augustine being ordained, and she is simply asking them to remember her when they are in church

---

[10]Vincenzo Fiocchi Nicolai, Fabrizio Bisconti and Danilo Mazzoleni, *The Christian Catacombs of Rome: History, Decoration, Inscriptions* (2nd edn, Schnell andSteiner, Regensburg, 2002), 64–66; and Robin N. Jensen, 'Dining with the Dead: From the Mensa to the Altar in Christian Late Antiquity' in Laurie Brink, Deborah Green and Walter de Gruyter (eds), *Commemorating the Dead: Texts and Artefacts in Context: Studies of Roman, Jewish and Christian Burials* (Walter de Gruyter, Berlin, 2008), 107-143.

[11]Sermon 51.3 in William B. Palardy (ed and trans), *St. Peter Chrysologus Selected Sermons Volume 2: The Fathers of the Church a New Translation*. Vol. 109 (CUA Press, Washington, D.C., 2004), 199.

[12]Stefan Heid, 'The Altar as Centre of Prayer and Priesthood in the Early Church' in Mariusz Biliniewcz (ed), *Agere in Persona Christi: Aspects of the Ministerial Priesthood* (Smenos, Wells, 2015), 27-53; and in Enrico Mazza, 'Tavola e Altare: Due Modi non Alternativi per Designare un Oggetto Liturgico' in Goffredo Boselli, (ed.), *L'Altare: Mistero di Presenza, Opera Dell'Arte* (Edizioni Qiqajon, Magnano, 2005), 66-68.

[13]On the Sacraments. Catechesis Five 2.7 in Lawrence J. Johnson (ed and trans), *Worship in the Early Church: An Anthology of Historical Sources* (Liturgical Press, Collegeville, MN, A Pueblo Book, 2009), 2.60.

[14]Confessions 9.11 in F. J. Sheed (trans), *Augustine: Confessions* (2nd edn, Hackett, Indianapolis, IN, 2006), 180.

near the altar, as this is the focus of popular prayer and devotion.[15] By the sixth century the altar was often considered to be the most sacred part of the church itself, a place of a special presence of God. When the faithful needed a special place to pray they usually prayed in front of the altar. Paradoxically, in this era when the altar was considered to be the main symbol of the presence of Christ, churches that were built at this time began to locate the altar further away from the faithful.[16] By the early Middle Ages the importance and holiness of the altar was often emphasized by decorative features such as a baldacchino, curtains, rails and rood screens.

---

[15]Other references to the altar as the preeminent presence of Christ can be found throughout the patristic period, e.g. Tertullian *On Penance* 9 in Johnson, *Worship in the Early Church* (Liturgical Press, Collegeville, MN, A Pueblo Book, 2009), 1.139; Gregory of Nazianzus, *Oration* 8.18 in *ibid.*, 2.144; Gregory of Nyssa, *Sermon on the Day of Lights on which Our Lord was Baptized* in *ibid.*, 2.155; Augustine *Sermon* 58.12 in *ibid.*, 3.59; in the anonymous treatise *De septem ordinibus ecclesiae* 5 in *ibid.*, 3.176; Caesarius of Arles *Sermon* 76.2 in *ibid.*, 4.107 and Gregory of Tours *History of the Franks* 2.34 in *ibid.*, 4.127.

[16]Iñiguez Herrero, *El Altar Cristiano*, 1.131–38.

2

Early Evidence of Liturgical Orientation

When looking at religion in general, we can note that some religious traditions promote prayer with worshippers facing in a particular direction. This was the case of many ancient religions, including the religion of Israel. In the Old Testament period there developed the custom of praying facing Jerusalem. This is something that differentiates Israel from the other religions in the ancient world, as this geographic type of orientation as found in Judaism (and later in Islam) was not as common as the astronomic type of orientation, that is more common in the classical religions and would be eventually adopted in Christianity.[17] The New Testament doesn't speak about facing in any particular direction to pray, and the texts that speak of the temple and the place of Christian prayer seem to be indifferent, if not outrightly hostile, to having a particular orientation in prayer.[18]

In early Christian texts we find some mention of orientation in prayer, for example Origen says this about having an astronomic consideration, for prayer (but he is referring to prayer at home as an early form of the liturgy of the hours and not to the eucharist):

A few words may now be said on the direction that one should face whilst at prayer. Since there are four directions, toward the north and

---

[17]Cyrille Vogel, 'L'Orientation vers l'Est du Célébrant et des Fidèles Pendant la Célébration Eucharistique' in L'Orient Syrien, 9 (1964), 5-6.

[18]See Matt 6.6; John 2.19; John 4.21-23; Acts 17.24; 1 Cor 3.16; 2 Cor 6.16 and Rev 21.10. I take these examples from Vogel, 'L'Orientation vers l'Est', 5.

the south, toward the rising of the sun and its setting, who would not immediately agree that the direction of the sunrise obviously indicates that we should make our prayer facing in that direction, as having the symbolic implication that the soul is facing the rising of the true light? ... It is by nature that the direction of the sunrise is to be favoured above the remaining directions and that the natural is to be upheld over the artificial.[19]

This is also reflected in the *Didascalia Apostolorum* 2.57 (probably dated to the third century):

Now in your congregations in the holy churches your gatherings should be conducted with good order. Appoint places for the brothers with care and gravity; the place of the presbyters should be separate, at the east end of the house, and the bishop's seat should be set among them, and the presbyters should sit with him. It is in another eastern part of the house that the laymen are to sit, for so it is required. The presbyters are to be seated in the eastern part of the house with the bishops, and then the laymen and then the women, so that when you stand up to pray the leaders should stand first, and then the laymen and subsequently the women. For it is required that your prayers should be directed towards the east, as you know what is written: 'Give glory to God who rides upon the heavens of heaven, towards the east.'[20]

The earliest official churches were those built under the patronage of the emperor Constantine in the fourth century, shortly after the legalization

---

[19]Origen, *On Prayer* 32 in Alistair Stewart-Sykes (ed and trans), *Tertullian, Cyprian and Origen: On The Lord's Prayer.* (Popular Patristics Series, SVS Press, Crestwood, NY, 2004), 211.

[20]*Didascalia Apostolorum* 2.57 in Alistair Stewart-Sykes (ed and trans), *The Didascalia Apostolorum: an English Version.* (*Studia Traditionis Theologiae: Explorations in Early and Medieval Theology*, Brepols, Turnhout, 2009), 174-175.

of Christianity. Only seven of the twenty Constantinian basilicas for which we have information are built to accommodate an *ad orientem* celebration of the eucharist.[21] Even in these cases the altar was never attached to the back wall of the church, which was the location of the cathedra.[22]

Paulinus of Nola (d. 431) writing about the basilica at Primuliacum comments on the fact that the new church was not facing west, as was the norm: 'The outlook of the basilica is not, after the usual fashion, towards the east, but faces the basilica of the blessed lord Felix, looking out upon his tomb.'[23] Church buildings seem to have been often built to take account of the sacred topography of the tombs of the martyrs or the holy places in the Holy Land rather than being built with an overriding concern of enabling the celebration of the eucharist with the priest facing *ad orientem*.

Recent studies of North African Christianity, have found many examples of late-fourth and early fifth century churches where the altar was in the main nave of the church and some examples where the altar was at the centre of the building.[24]

However as time went by the idea of having the church built in such a way as to facilitate *ad orientem* celebrations of the eucharist gradually became a consideration and by the fifth century the majority (but not all) churches faced east.[25] However St Peter's Basilica, the most famous church in Christendom, was not built to facilitate *ad orientem* worship, so that even today in the new basilica, the Pope is celebrating *ad orientem* when he celebrates *versus populum* on the main altar of the basilica. In the fifth century Pope St Leo the Great preached against those superstitious

---

[21]See Vogel, 'L'Orientation vers l'Est', 14.

[22]See *ibid.*, 16.

[23]Letter 32.13 in Patrick Gerard Walsh (ed and trans), *Letters of St. Paulinus of Nola*, Vol. 2 (*Ancient Christian Writers* Vol. 36, Paulist Press, Mahwah, NJ, 1966), 147.

[24]Robin M. Jensen, 'Recovering Ancient Ecclesiology: The Place of the Altar and the Orientation of Prayer in the Early Latin Church' in *Worship* 89 (2015), 104-108.

[25]See Vogel, 'L'Orientation vers l'Est', 22.

Roman Christians, who were accustomed to make a prayer facing the rising sun in the east as they are entering St Peter's Basilica, giving their back to the *Confessio* of St Peter. In his homily for Christmas Day in 451 he says that:

> From such customs as this has the following godlessness been engendered, where the sun–as it rises at daybreak–would be worshipped from the higher elevations by certain sillier people. Even some Christians think that they behave devoutly when, before arriving at the basilica of the blessed Apostle Peter (which has been dedicated to the one living and true God), they climb the steps which go up to the platform on the upper level, turn themselves around towards the rising sun and bow down to honour its shining disk.[26]

Some scholars have written about St Augustine's invitation to the assembly to '*conversi ad Dominum*' (turn towards the Lord), that is found at the end of three of his sermons. This is sometimes understood to be an invitation to the assembly physically to face east for the eucharistic prayer, which the authors assume to have been celebrated *ad orientem*.[27] Here perhaps there is a tendency to overemphasize the evidence as it comes from St Augustine himself. However, this is a phrase that is used only very rarely by Augustine in his sermons. Vogel makes the point that the phrase is unclear and we are not really sure what St Augustine is referring to.[28] More significantly Jensen, an expert in the intersection of Christian art and liturgy, travelled to Hippo in North Africa and examined the still-visible archaeological remains of St Augustine's church in person. Her analysis has shown that Augustine's invitation is more than likely not literal as:

---

[26]Sermon 27, In nativitate Domini 7.4 in Jane P. Freeland and Agnes J. Conway (eds and trans), *Leo The Great: Sermons* (*Fathers of the Church* Vol. 93, CUA Press, Washington D.C., 1996), 113.
[27]This is the argument, for example in Lang, *Turning Towards the Lord*, 51-52 and in Joseph Ratzinger, *The Spirit of the Liturgy*, (trans John Saward, Ignatius Press, San Francisco, 2000), 82–85.
[28]See Vogel, 'L'Orientation vers l'Est', 11-12.

In Hippo, such an instruction, presumably pronounced at the end of a sermon and before the dismissal of the catechumens and the prayer of the faithful, would have required the compliant congregation to turn nearly 135 degrees in a clockwise direction to face the right rear corner of the church building.[29]

This confrontation of the textual evidence with archaeological adds an important level to analysis. But it only goes to prove once again, how fragmentary our grasp of the past is and the danger of reading our own preferences and biases into the evidence at our disposal and of placing too much emphasis on a single phrase.

We can see clear evidence of the spread of *ad orientem* worship in *Ordo Romanus Primus*. The *Ordines Romani* are a very important body of work for understanding the history of the Roman rite; they consist of liturgical manuals that describe the papal liturgies. These were compiled by visitors to Rome, who wished to bring home the traditions of the papal liturgy.[30] *Ordo Romanus Primus* is the first of these and describes the papal liturgy as it was celebrated towards the end of the seventh century. The description of the collect or opening prayer of the mass is particularly enlightening. There are two variants of this text: the first is the Roman recension which simply states:

When they are finishing [the Kyrie], the pope starts the 'Glory to God in the highest,' if it is the season for it, and he does not sit down until they have said Amen after the first prayer.[31]

---

[29]Jensen, 'Recovering Ancient Ecclesiology', 117.

[30]For more on the *Ordines Romani* see Cyrille Vogel, *Medieval Liturgy: An Introduction to the Sources* (William Storey and Niels Rasmussen (ed and trans), The Pastoral Press, Portland, OR, 1986), 135-224 and Éric Palazzo, *A History of Liturgical Books: From the Beginning to the Thirteenth Century* (Madeleine Beaumont (trans), A Pueblo Book, Liturgical Press, Collegeville, MN, 1998), 175-185.

[31]My translation of OR I, 53 from Michel Andrieu, *Les Ordines Romani du Haut Moyen Age* Vol 2 *Les Textes: Ordines I-XIII Spicilegium Sacrum Lovaniense* Vol. 23 (Spicilegium, Louvain, 1960), 84-85.

However the Gallican recension of the same text reads very differently:

> When they have finished [the Kyrie], the pope turns to the people and begins 'Glory to God in the highest.' He turns to face east immediately until they have finished. Then he turns to face the people again and he says 'Peace be with you' and turning east again he says 'Let us pray' and the prayer. At the conclusion of the prayer he sits down. Bishops and presbyters also sit down.[32]

This is evidence of a concern with the orientation of prayer in the Gallican area that this edition came from. In the history of the liturgy in the west a great emphasis is placed on the formation of the Roman and Gallican rites and the eventual merger of these into one composite rite that basically remains to this day as the nucleus of the Roman rite.[33]

---

[32]I take this translation from Alan Griffiths, *Ordo Romanus Primus: Latin Text and Translations with Introduction and Notes* (Alcuin/GROW Joint Liturgical Studies 73, Hymns Ancient & Modern, Norwich, 2012), 41. Note that I have slightly modified the translation as Griffiths is using a version of the text based on a harmonization of both the Roman and the Gallican recensions.

[33]I trace this development in *The Eucharist in Pre-Norman Ireland*, 40-50.

3

Historical Background: The Middle Ages

By the middle ages the practice of celebrating mass *ad orientem* had become more or less universal. Medieval church architecture and the iconographic programming of churches and ecclesial centres show an intricate grasp of the issue of light 'as the manifestation of God' and in that context the rising of the sun in the east and its shining on eastern facing altars was undoubtedly a consideration in the design of churches.[34] In the early ninth century, Amalarius of Metz, one of the principal medieval authors on the liturgy, gave a very detailed explanation of the priest praying *ad orientem* when celebrating the mass.[35]

However, even in this period it seems that there may have been exceptions. Some recent work on Anglo-Saxon churches has suggested that the altar may have stood between the sanctuary and nave with a bench for the clergy in the centre of the apse. This would imply that the priest would have celebrated the eucharist facing the people.[36] In

---

[34]Sharon Gerstel and Michael Cothren, 'The Iconography of Light' in Colum Hourihane (ed), *The Routledge Companion to Medieval Iconography* (Routledge, London, 2016), 469.

[35]See 'On the Liturgy 3.9' in Eric Knibbs (ed. and trans.), *Amalar of Metz: On the Liturgy, Volume II: Books 3-4* (Dumbarton Oaks Medieval Library Vol. 36, Harvard University Press, Harvard, MA, 2014), 60-65.

[36]David Parsons, *Liturgy and Architecture in the Middle Ages* (Friends of Deerhurst Church, Deerhurst, 1989), 18-21. More research needs to be done in order to know how widespread this arrangement was. For a summary of the evidence as the state of study now stands, see David Parsons, 'Sacrarium Ablution Drains in Early Medieval Churches' in L. A. S. Butler and R. K. Morris (eds), *The Anglo-Saxon Church: Papers on History, Architecture and Archaeology in Honour of Dr. H.M. Taylor* (CBA Research Report 60, Council for British Archaeology, London, 1986), 105-120. This theory has been more recently supported by Carol F. Davidson, 'Change and Change

some cases mass was celebrated above the people, in the twelfth century church of St Gall in France, there are records of two round towers with altars to the archangels St Michael and St Gabriel.[37]

By the late Middle Ages, the altar was often almost completely hidden from the sight of the people and the central prayer of the Sunday eucharistic liturgy was carried out almost in secret outside of the sight and hearing of the assembly. However this does not necessarily imply that the people were totally separated from the liturgical action. While the high altar might have been distant, the laity often had a more intimate liturgical experience at votive masses and weekday eucharistic liturgies at the various side-altars that were present in most churches. These celebrations had a much more popular dimension, oftentimes with the laity crowded around the altar for the celebration.[38]

Even in the Middle Ages the possibility of viewing what was happening on the altar at mass was often considered to be important. The Royal Abbey Church at Saint-Denis (on the outskirts of Paris) was one of the most significant church buildings of this period and many identify this church as being the first church in the Gothic style of church architecture. Abbot Suger, who masterminded its construction, has left an account of its consecration in 1144. The high point of the celebration

---

Back: the Development of English Parish Church Chancels' in R. N. Swanson (ed), *Continuity and Change in Christian Worship: Papers Read at the 1997 Summer Meeting and the 1998 Winter Meeting of the Ecclesiastical History Society* (The Boydell Press, Woodbridge, Suffolk, 1999), 75-76. Lara gives another example from slightly later Anglo-Norman cathedrals where the altar was suspended above the congregation on a wooden bridge, so that the people were under the altar and looking up at priest as he celebrated. See Jaime Lara, '*Versus Populum* Revisited', in *Worship* 68 (1994), 218.

[37]Walter Horn and E. Born, *The Plan of St. Gall* (Vol I, University of California Press, Berkley, CA, 1979), 129, 166. It has even been proposed that the famous medieval Round Towers that dot many Irish ecclesial sites were in fact churches where mass was celebrated above the church complex; see Tadhg O'Keeffe, *Ireland's Round Towers* (Tempus, Stroud, 2004), 106, but cf. my own *Eucharist in Pre-Norman Ireland*, 102-103, for some contrary opinions.

[38]Eamon Duffy, *The Stripping of the Altars: Traditional Religion in England 1400–1580* (2nd edn, Yale University Press, New Haven, CT, 2005), 111–16. For examples of various medieval altars see, Justin E. A. Kroesen and Victor M. Schmidt (eds), *The Altar and its Environment 1150-1400* (*Studies in the Visual Culture of the Middle Ages* Vol. 4, Brepols, Turnhout, 2009).

was a harmonized celebration of the mass by the 19 consecrating bishops, each presiding at an individual mass on 19 separate altars, placed in a semi-circle on two levels around the high altar. Suger tells us:

> After the consecration of the altars all these [dignitaries] performed a solemn celebration of masses, both in the upper choir and in the crypt, so festively, so solemnly, so different and yet so concordantly, so close [to one another] and so joyfully that their song, delightful by its consonance and unified harmony, was deemed a symphony angelic rather than human.[39]

Here seeing what was happening is very important. Coincidentally one of the most famous artistic renditions of a medieval mass is also from this church, albeit from about four hundred years after Abbot Suger. The Master of Saint Giles painted the famous picture 'The Mass of St Giles' around the year 1500 and set the mass in the church of Saint-Denis. The painting, now in London's National Gallery, shows a scene from the life of St Giles. The King (identified as Charles Martel) kneeling on the left has a perfect view of all the action on the altar. But the other people in the picture can peek through the curtain on the east side of the altar, so that the mass being celebrated there is virtually *versus populum*.[40]

Obviously there is a limit to what can be deduced from Suger's account and from this painting. The clergy were always close to the altar and other social élites had a better chance of being closer to the altar than the poor, having private chapels in their homes and even having private

---

[39]*De Consecratione ecclesiae Sancti Dionysii VII* in Erwin Panofsky (ed and trans), *Abbot Suger on the Abbey-Church of Saint-Denis and its Art Treasures* (Princeton University Press, Princeton, NJ, 1946), 118-121.

[40]For more details on this image and examples of other similar images from different parts of Europe, many showing people very close to the altar see Caroline Walker Bynum, 'Seeing and Seeing Beyond: The Mass of St. Gregory in the Fifteenth Century' in Jeffrey F. Hamburger and Anne-Marie Bouche (eds), *The Mind's Eye: Art and Theological Argument in the Middle Ages* (Princeton University Press, Princeton, NJ, 2006), 208-240.

chapels in some churches. Yet even the poor had a desire to be close to the altar and many of the guilds and confraternities that emerged in the Middle Ages had their own chapels and chaplains in order to allow their members better access to the altar that was on a par with the rich.[41]

Figure One: The Mass of Saint Giles by the Master of Saint Giles about 1500 from The National Gallery, London[42]

---

[41]Jon Henderson, Piety and Charity in *Late Medieval Florence* (2nd edn, University of Chicago Press, Chicago, IL, 1997), 35.

[42]Image in public domain and available at http://commons.wikimedia.org/wiki/File:Massgiles.jpg

Another medieval development that has some bearing on our considerations is the gradual development of a 'ritual independence' of the eucharist species from the actual celebration.[43] Popular devotion became centred on the eucharistic species which often had no direct relationship with the altar itself.[44] This desire to see and 'gaze on the Body of Christ with their own bodily eyes'[45] was to become a central aspect of western catholic piety until our own days. Over time, devotions such as the festival of Corpus Christi developed and now the eucharistic bread was most visible to people and received most devotion not during the liturgy of the eucharist itself, but in processions and when the Blessed Sacrament was exposed for worship.[46]

---

[43]G.J.C. Snoek, *Medieval Piety from Relics to the Eucharist a Process of Mutual Interaction* (*Studies in the History of Christian Thought*, Vol. 63, Brill, Leiden,1995), xi.

[44]Nathan Mitchell, *Cult and Controversy: The Worship of the Eucharist Outside Mass* (Pueblo, New York, 1982), 163.

[45]Enrico Mazza (trans Matthew J. O'Connell), *The Celebration of the Eucharist: The Origins of the Rite and the Development of its Interpretation* (Liturgical Press, Collegeville, MN, 1999), 195.

[46]For the development of this phenomenon in the Middle Ages, see Miri Rubin, *Corpus Christi: The Eucharist in Late Medieval Culture* (Cambridge University Press, Cambridge, 1991), 135-139.

4

The Reformation and Trent to Vatican II

The Reformation was to see some radical changes in worship practices in the Christian west.[47] Many of these changes were not in keeping with the tradition of the liturgy and sacramental practice became very poor among many Christians influenced by the reformers. Shortly afterwards at the Council of Trent, the Catholic Church condemned many of these innovations. Yet not all of the liturgical developments among the reformers were negative and each needs to be analyzed by itself to evaluate its merits.[48]

Eucharistic practice in protestantism did depart radically from the catholic practice, to the degree that the Catholic Church has taught that the very sacrament of the eucharist itself does not validly exist in protestantism. On the protestant side there was a debate on how often the eucharist or Lord's supper ought to be celebrated, with many protestant communities celebrating it on only a limited number of occasions during the year.[49] As protestantism is not a single movement, it is not surprising that there is no single united position on the orientation of the eucharist

---

[47]For a brief summary of the liturgical developments in see P. Jounel, 'From the Council of Trent to Vatican Council II' in A. G. Martimort (ed), *The Church at Prayer Volume I: Principles of the Liturgy* (Liturgical Press, Collegeville, MN, 1987), 64-65; for a more comprehensive account see James White, *Protestant Worship: Traditions in Transition* (Westminster John Knox Press, Louisville, KY, 1989).

[48]For example the Reformation promoted liturgical worship in the vernacular, something that the Catholic Church was eventually to adopt after Vatican II. See my 'Words of Salvation', 59-60.

[49]Susan J. White, 'Sacraments in the Reformation Churches', in Peter E. Fink, *The New Dictionary of Sacramental Worship* (Liturgical Press, Collegeville, MN, 2000), 1132–1133.

or celebration of the Lord's supper. But there are a few individual contributions to the debate. In 1526 in his *Preface to the German Mass* Luther suggested *versus populum* in this manner:

> We retain the vestments, altar and candles until they are used up or we are pleased to make a change. But we do not oppose anyone who would do otherwise. In the true Mass, however, of real Christians, the altar should not remain where it is, and the priest should always face the people as Christ doubtless did in the Last Supper.[50]

However it seems that while this was recommended, many Lutherans regarded this more in the way of a suggestion than a rule. Some Lutheran parishes followed this practice and others continued to celebrate *ad orientem* with some new altars even being built in the traditional style facilitating only *ad orientem* liturgies.[51] In the Church of England the table became free-standing, but over time generally returned to the east wall. Initially the priest stood on the north side and celebrated from that side of the table.[52] Many Anglican services followed the rubric of the 1662 Book of Common Prayer which, following the 1552 text, stated that '*the priest, standing at the north side of the table, shall say the Lord's Prayer with the Collect following*.' Until the nineteenth century the 'altar' was usually a wooden table and, while its position had not been initially fixed in the churches, it gradually became to be placed on the east wall of the church allowing the celebrant to preside over the liturgy from

---

[50]Martin Luther, 'German Mass, 1526' in Ulrich S. Leupold (ed), Paul Zeller Strodach (trans), *Liturgy and Hymns* (vol. 53 of *Luther's Works*, American Edition, Jaroslav Pelikan and Helmut T. Lehmann (eds), Fortress, Philadelphia, 1965), 69.

[51]Andrew Spicer, 'Sites of the Eucharist' in Lee Palmer Wandel (ed), *A Companion to the Eucharist in the Reformation* (Brill, Leiden, 2013), 337-339.

[52]For more on the various developments of Anglican practice in the sixteenth and seventeenth century see Ronald Jasper, *The Position of the Celebrant at the Eucharist* (Alcuin Club pamphlet XVI , Mowbray, London, 1959), 19-23.

the short north side.[53]John Henry Newman, for example, celebrated the eucharist at the north side of the altar in the church of St. Mary the Virgin at Oxford prior to entering the Catholic Church.[54] But this north side position was to dwindle greatly in the nineteenth century. In 1839 the Cambridge Camden Society was founded. This group of architects was to become very influential in world Anglicanism and they advocated that Anglican churches adopt an idealized Gothic architecture and many of the liturgical practices of medieval catholicism, including a return to *ad orientem* worship and the use of stone altars. This practice was to remain popular until the Liturgical Movement of the twentieth century when most Anglican churches adopted *versus populum* worship.[55]

The reformed churches in Scotland, Holland and France removed all traces of the existing altars when they inherited catholic churches and there were no permanent altars in their newly-built churches.[56] In the churches influenced by Calvin the altar was replaced by a simple 'communion table' which was not a permanent fixture in the church.[57]

Although the Council of Trent is often cited as a major cause of the stabilization of the liturgy in the Roman rite, however this stability was one of ritual texts and standardized printed liturgical books, such as the Roman Missal.[58] The liturgical renewal in the wake of Trent gave a

---

[53]Colin Buchanan, 'The Position of the President Revisited: Exploring an Historical Anglican Bypath' in *Studia Liturgica* 35(2005), 121.

[54]*Ibid.*

[55]James White, 'Prayer Book Architecture' in Charles Hefling and Cynthia Shattuck (eds), *The Oxford Guide to the Book of Common Prayer: a Worldwide Survey* (Oxford University Press, Oxford, 2006), 106-115. For more on the different traditions of Anglican worship see Bryan Spinks, 'Anglicans and Dissenters' in Geoffrey Wainwright and Karen N. Westerfield Tucker (eds), *The Oxford History of Christian Worship* (Oxford University Press, 2006) 493-533.

[56]Spicer, 'Sites of the Eucharist', 343.

[57]Nathan Mitchell, 'Reforms, Protestant and Catholic' in Wainwright and Westerfield Tucker (eds), *The Oxford History of Christian Worship*, 324.

[58]For the history of the Roman Missal between the Council of Trent and Vatican II see Paul Gunter, '*Sacerdos Paratus and Populo Congrato*: the Historical Development of the Roman Missal' in Janet Rutherford and James O'Brien (eds), *Benedict XVI and the Roman Missal. Proceedings of*

special importance in people's spirituality to their actually being able to see the celebration of the liturgy at the altar and one of the main features of churches built after the Council of Trent was the disappearance of the choir. This meant that the church was no longer a sort of shrine which contained a hidden high altar divided from the common nave by the choir. Instead churches were now built based on 'the concept of one unified liturgical space, an altar visible to all, and acoustics favourable to preaching.'[59] This reform was pioneered by the new Jesuit religious order. One of the novelties of the Jesuits was that as an order they did not have an obligation to pray the liturgy of the Hours in community and therefore their churches did not have a choir. Pastorally they soon realized the value of allowing people to see the actual celebration of the eucharist. The eucharist was still celebrated *ad orientem*, and the assembly could not properly see the sacramental elements when they were placed on the altar. But in this new liturgical aesthetic the altar was placed at the focal point of the church so that everybody could visually participate in the eucharistic liturgy, by looking at the priest as he presided at the altar. The famous mid-sixteenth century Jesuit church of the Gesù in Rome served as the main exemplar of this new form of church architecture. Here the altar is very prominently placed in the centre of the sanctuary so that it is visible to the whole assembly.[60] The Baroque period complemented the Post-Tridentine view of the altar as the visual focal point of the church. This style emphasized the position of the altar by adding magnificent

---

the Fourth Fota International Liturgy Conference 2012 (Four Courts Press, Dublin, 2013), 40-69. But this history of the missal must be complemented by a history of the liturgy as a whole, see White, *Roman Catholic Worship*. For a facsimile of the Roman Missal as published as a result of the liturgical renewal promoted by the Council of Trent see Manlio Soldi and A. M. Triacca, (eds), *Missale Romanum: Editio Princeps* (1570) (Libreria Editrice Vaticana, Rome, 1998).

[59]White, *Roman Catholic Worship*, 3.

[60]*Ibid*, 2–5. Note however that the centrality of the high altar in the church of Gesù today is not quite as obvious as when the church was built due to the various ornamental additions to the church over the centuries. For more on this church see T. H. Fokker, 'The First Baroque Church in Rome' in *The Art Bulletin*, 15 (1933): 230–49.

reredos as backdrops to the altar.[61] So profound was the new liturgical aesthetic introduced by the Jesuits, that most Catholic churches built in the English-speaking world between Catholic emancipation and Vatican II followed the design of Gesù at least with respect to the location and visual prominence of the altar.

Figure Two: Interior of the Church of the Royal Collegiate Church of Saint Hippolytus, Cordoba, Spain[62]

---

[61]For a study on a particular geographical area and how the altars were not just the place to perform the eucharistic liturgy but formed a visual catechism so that people could contemplate the mysteries of the faith, see Justin E. A. Kroesen, *Staging the Liturgy: The Medieval Altarpiece in the Iberian Peninsula* (Peeters, Leuven, 2009).

[62]Image in the public domain and available at https://commons.wikimedia.org/wiki/File:Interior_de_la_iglesia_de_San_Hipólito_de_Córdoba.JPG N.B although the Church of the Gesù in Rome was the archetype of the new architectural style pioneered by the Jesuits, this church became heavily ornamented and this example from the Jesuit church in Cordoba gives a better idea of the plain style centred on the altar of the original Gesù. Diarmaid MacCulloch, *The Reformation: A History* (Viking Penguin, New York, 2003), 315.

However we should also note that there were other opinions in the wake of the Council of Trent. Shortly after the Council, St Charles Borromeo codified his understanding of the best way to celebrate the liturgy as envisioned by Trent. In 1577 he published his *Instructiones fabricae et supellectilis ecclesiasticae* where he outlined how the church should be built in order best to celebrate the liturgy. Here he also proposed that it is best for the priest to celebrate the eucharist 'from the high altar facing the people' [*sacerdote versa ad populum facie missae sacrum in altari maiori fieri solet*].[63] While this proposal of Borromeo was not widely adopted, it does show that it was still a live issue in the time after the Council of Trent.

Another development at this time was that tabernacles came to be placed on altars, so that the main altar often became a sort of throne for the tabernacle, rather than being the place for the celebration of the eucharist.[64] There had been forerunners of the tabernacle for centuries in the form of pyxes or eucharistic doves. But in the wake of the Council of Trent, when Gilbert, the Bishop of Verona, advocated the practice of reserving the eucharist in a tabernacle on the altar, his friend, St Charles Borromeo, extended this practice in most of the north of Italy (he was more successful with this proposal than that of *versus populum* celebrations) and Pope Paul V encouraged this practice in Rome. From there it passed to the whole world. But in fact it was not mandatory until 1863 when the Sacred Congregation for Rites prohibited the reservation of the eucharist apart from the altar.[65] So after the Council of Trent,

---

[63]*Instructiones fabricae et supellectilis ecclesiasticae* 10. For more background see John W. O'Malley, *Trent: What Happened at the Council* (Belknap Press of Harvard University, Cambridge, MA, 2013), 261. An examination of the original texts and further reflections on this passage is provided by Jonathan Day's blog post at http://www.praytellblog.com/index.php/2014/11/26/celebration-facing-the-people-a-centuries-old-practice/

[64]John F. Baldovin, *Bread of Life, Cup of Salvation: Understanding the Mass* (Rowman & Littlefield, A Sheed & Ward Book, Lanham, MD, 2003), 58.

[65]On August 21, 1863 the prefect of the Sacred Congregation of Rites wrote to the Belgian bishops forbidding the further use of aumbries or towers for reservation of the Blessed Sacrament and mandated that only tabernacles on altars be used, Peter F. Anson (rev and ed Thomas F. Crofts-

although there was a renewed emphasis on seeing the eucharistic liturgy and although many altar screens were removed to provide a clear line of vision to the altar, the centre of the eucharistic liturgy was still far from the experience of many people. The words of the mass were not only in Latin, but the central part of the anaphora continued to be prayed in a low voice that was inaudible from the assembly.[66] Additionally many of the central signs of the liturgy were invisible to the assembly, such as, for example, the breaking of the bread, the action that was synonymous with the eucharist in the Acts of the Apostles was now never seen by the assembly and no one other than a priest ever saw a broken piece of the eucharistic bread in any liturgy.[67]

Figure Three: Detail of The Foundation Mass of the Order of Trinitarians by Juan Carreño de Miranda, 1665[68]

Fraser and H. A. Reinhold), *Churches their Plan and Furnishing* (Bruce, Milwaukee, WI, 1948), 90.

[66]Robert F. Taft, 'Was the Eucharistic Anaphora Recited Secretly or Aloud? The Ancient Tradition and what became of it' in Roberta R. Ervine (ed), *Worship Traditions in Armenia and the Neighboring Christian East: An International Symposium in Honor of the Fortieth Anniversary of St Nersess Armenian Seminary* (St. Vladimir's Seminary Press, Crestwood, NY, 2006), 15–57.

[67]Barry M. Craig, *Fractio Panis: A History of the Breaking of Bread in the Roman Rite* (Studia Anselmiana, Rome, 2011), 229.

[68]La Messe de fondation de l'ordre des Trinitaires RF1964-36. Photo © RMN-Grand Palais

I conclude this section with reference to two representative images (many more could have been chosen), which together give some idea how congregations from different countries and social backgrounds desired to be close to the altar and to see what was happening during the eucharistic prayer. Figure Three shows the lower half of *The Foundation Mass of the Order of Trinitarians*. This monumental canvas was painted by Juan Carreño de Miranda in 1665 for the high altar of the Trinitarian church at Pamplona. It shows St John of Matha celebrating his first mass, where he has a vision that inspires him to found the Trinitarian Order. For the purposes of this study we are interested in the celebration of the mass. The altar is clearly not *versus populum* but the assembly is crowded around the altar, with some of the congregation being closer to the altar than the altar servers.

Figure Four (overleaf) is in the context of a nineteenth-century Irish station mass. This eucharist celebrated in one of the poorest parts of Europe could not be further removed from high society and the liturgical *avant-garde*. Yet here too the humble peasants crowd around the altar, finding their closeness to the altar to be a high point in their spiritual lives.

(Musée du Louvre) / Gérad Blot. Used with permission.

**Figure Four: Mass in a Connemara Cabin
by Aloysius O'Kelly, c.1883[69]**

---

[69]   Photo © National Gallery of Ireland, used with the permission of the National Gallery of
Ireland, the Parish of St. Patrick's, Cowgate, Edinburgh and the R.C. Archdiocese of Edinburgh.

5

20th Century Adoption of *versus populum* Orientation

The Liturgical Movement was one of the most important themes in catholicism in the 20th century. It was primarily a movement that sought to put the liturgy back at the centre of the spiritual lives of catholics. Although the name Liturgical Movement implies a single movement, in fact this was not a single movement with a single leadership. It was centred on different institutions and individuals, each of whom had different goals and particular emphases of common themes. The particular leader to have emphasized the adoption of *versus populum* celebration was Romano Guardini.

Romano Guardini (1885-1968) was one of the most influential pastoral theologians of the first half of the twentieth century, and he helped lay the foundations for the liturgical renewal of the second Vatican Council.[70] He grew up with the pious formation proper to that time, where one was expected to pray at liturgy and especially at mass, but there never was much of an idea that the actual participation in the mass could be of value in and of itself. Strange as it may seem to us today, the church's precept to attend mass on Sunday was basically understood as obligating catholics to be physically present in their parish church while mass was being celebrated and had no reference to participation

---

[70]For an introduction to his contribution to the liturgical renewal of the twentieth century see Robert A. Krieg, *Romano Guardini: A Precursor of Vatican II* (University of Notre Dame Press, Notre Dame, IN, 1997), 70-90.

in the actual liturgical celebration.[71] As a theology student Guardini worshipped at the monastery of Beuron. He already had a strong prayer life, which helped him in his difficult upbringing and in his struggle against depression, but in this monastery he discovered that the liturgy was not simply a place to pray, but prayer itself, that it was possible to worship God by participating in the liturgy, rather than by simply attending the liturgy and praying while physically present in the liturgy. Guardini benefited from coming into contact with one of the centres of the Liturgical Movement, which up until then had been mainly a monastic movement. But while Guardini loved what he had found in the monastery, he saw that his own vocation was to be a diocesan priest and not a monk. So he was very instrumental in bringing the renewal that he had found in the monastery to parish life. Guardini was particularly involved in the youth ministry of the *Jugendbewegung* which had started in the aftermath of World War I; and was trying to give meaning to young people and provide an alternative to the anti-Christian totalitarian movements in Germany that eventually gave birth to Nazism and World War II. In a later letter he expresses the kernel of his concerns:

> As I see it, typical nineteenth century man was no longer able to perform this act [the liturgical act]; in fact he was unaware of its existence. Religious conduct was to him an individual inward manner which in the 'liturgy' took on the character of an official, public ceremonial. But the sense of the liturgical action was thereby lost. The faithful did not perform a proper liturgical act at all, it was simply a private and inward act, surrounded by ceremonial and not infrequently accompanied by a feeling that the ceremonial was really a disturbing factor. From that point of view the efforts of those

---

[71]For example see the treatment of 'attendance at Holy Mass' in Heribert Jone, *Moral Theology* (translated and updated to the Customs of the United States by Urban Adelman, Newman Press, Westminster, MD, 1961), 123-126.

who concerned themselves with the liturgy must have appeared as peculiarities of aesthetes who lacked Christian sincerity.[72]

Guardini saw that one of the ways to bridge the gap between the person of today and the liturgy was to celebrate the eucharist *versus populum*. Guardini probably was inspired by the example of Pius Parsch. Parsch was the apostle of the Liturgical Movement in Austria. He had been a chaplain during World War I and had been amazed by soldiers' lack of devotion and religious sensibility. After the war he was given the pastoral care of St Gertrude's chapel, and in 1935 he reordered the church with an altar that allowed *versus populum* celebrations.[73] He aimed at fostering an active participation of the laity in the liturgy. Guardini, in his turn, was to become one of the main proponents of this practice on the parish level, particularly in youth ministry. Guardini succeeded in popularizing the practice so that the celebration of the eucharist *versus populum* became quite widespread in German-speaking areas. For an example of how this looked see the front cover illustration, which is a photo of a family mass in the Von Trapp family (of *The Sound of Music* fame) with the priest facing the assembly.

Prior to Vatican II there was no official adoption of *versus populum* celebrations. However the 1956 reform of the liturgies of Holy Week did contain some minor developments in the official revised rites that gave consideration to the assembly actually being able to see what was happening. The blessing of the palms at Palm Sunday was now done on a small table with the priest facing the people and not with his back to them. The procession with the palms also concluded with a new prayer

---

[72]Guardini's 1963 'Open Letter to the Third German Liturgical Conference' is published in English translation in Paul Bradshaw and John Melloh, *Foundations in Ritual Studies: A Reader for Students of Christian Worship* (Baker, Grand Rapids, MI, 2007), 4.

[73]Alcuin Reid, *The Organic Development of the Liturgy: The Principles of Liturgical Reform to the Twentieth Century Liturgical Movement Prior to the Second Vatican Council* (St. Michael's Abbey Press, Farnborough, 2004), 100.

which was, again, facing the people. Similarly the revised rites of the Easter vigil prescribed that the baptismal water be blessed in a basin in the sanctuary, with the priest facing the people and with his back to the high altar.[74]

I do not want to give a false impression that *versus populum* was very popular throughout the Liturgical Movement prior to Vatican II. In the 1960s the vast majority of catholic masses were still celebrated *ad orientem*; and only a very few priests, mainly those in the circles of the Liturgical Movement and influenced by Guardini celebrated *versus populum*. This is well illustrated by a parallel reform. Prior to Vatican II there was a Vernacular Society active in both England and the United States promoting the adoption of the vernacular in the celebration of the sacraments, and thousands of English speakers desired strongly that the liturgy should be in their native language and wrote to Archbishop Bugnini petitioning for the use of the vernacular in the liturgy.[75] But there was no comparable popular movement campaigning in favour of *versus populum*.

[74]A very critical analysis of these points can be found in the detailed web post of Stefano Carusi, 'The Reform of Holy Week in the Years 1951-1956 from Liturgy to Theology by Way of the Statements of Certain Leading Thinkers (Annibale Bugnini, Carlo Braga, Ferdinando Antonelli).' This was originally in Italian but a translation is available at http://rorate-caeli.blogspot.com/2015/04/the-reform-of-holy-week-in-years-1951.html For more on this revision in general see Nicola Giampietro, *The Development of the Liturgical Reform as Seen by Cardinal Ferdinando Antonelli from 1948 to 1970* (Roman Catholic Books, Fort Collins, 2009), 15-72.
[75]Keith F. Pecklers, *Dynamic Equivalence: The Living Language of Christian Worship* (a Pueblo Book, Liturgical Press, Collegeville, MN, 2003), 158.

6

Vatican II

Contemporary authors who express a preference for *ad orientem* celebration of the eucharist often point out that Vatican II's *Sacrosanctum Concilium* (henceforth SC) or Decree on the Sacred liturgy does not mention the position of the altar.[76] This may be true in a strict sense, but when we examine this claim in more detail, the picture is not quite as clear as is sometimes made out. The first point that needs to be stressed is that by the time of Vatican II there was a general agreement that the liturgy needed to be renewed. The church was emerging from two World Wars and something had to be done to reach contemporary people who no longer looked to the church for answers to life's problems. In the words of the young Ratzinger: 'the liturgy had become a rigid, fixed and firmly encrusted system … out of touch with genuine piety… [Where the people] were united with the priest only by being in the same church with him.'[77]

St John XXIII saw that the reform of the liturgy carried out by his predecessors (such as St Pius X's emphasis on frequent communion and Pius XII's renewal of Holy Week) as something that needed to continue. However, he did not have a particularly long pontificate and it is without doubt that calling an Ecumenical Council was its main achievement. He did some minor work on the liturgy (such as promulgating a lightly edited edition of the missal of St Pius V), but, once he had called the

---

[76]E.g. Lang, *Turning Towards the Lord*, 21.

[77]Joseph Ratzinger, *Theological Highlights of Vatican II* (Paulist Press, Mahwah, NJ, 1966, new edn. 2009), 131-132.

second Vatican Council, he envisioned that the Council would provide a more complete direction for the reform of the liturgy. At Vatican II 'the more important principles governing a general liturgical reform should be laid before the members of the hierarchy at the forthcoming ecumenical council.'[78] But rather than mandating specific reforms on the floor of St Peter's during the Council or by compiling explicit and exhaustive suggestions in the text of the Constitution on the Liturgy, John XXIII's goal was that once a direction for reform was agreed upon at the Council, the specific reforms could be carried out by the Pope and the various offices of the Holy See.[79] With this background, it is more important to understand that the goal of Vatican II was to agree upon principles of liturgical reform rather than propose actual reforms. In the end, the fathers of the council were unable to restrain themselves and they did insert some specific reforms into the Constitution. However these specific reforms were not as important as the principles of reform that governed the whole liturgical renewal which was to be carried out by the Holy See after the Council finished (much as had been the case in the liturgical reform carried out in the wake of the Council of Trent under the guidance of St Pius V).

SC restated the Catholic Church's understanding that the liturgy contains both immutable, divinely instituted elements and elements that are subject to change. Obviously the immutable elements have no need of renewal and the church is not free to alter them. But the other elements 'not only may but ought to be changed with the passage of time if they have suffered from the intrusion of anything out of harmony with the inner nature of the liturgy or have become pointless' (*SC* 21). The decree

---

[78]*Rubricarum instructum* in *Acta Apostolica Sedes* 52 (1960), 594 (English trans from Richstatter, *New Style, New Spirit*, 50).

[79]Cipriano Vagagini, 'Fundamental Ideal of the Constitution' in William Baraúna (ed), *The Liturgy of Vatican II: A Symposium in Two Volumes* (English Edition ed Jovian Lang, Franciscan Herald Press, Chicago, IL, 1966), 1:96–98; and Annibale Bugnini, *The Reform of the Liturgy: 1948 – 1975* (trans Matthew J. O'Connell, Liturgical Press, Collegeville, MN, 1990), 39-48.

goes on to say that 'in this Renewal both the texts and rites should be so drawn up that they express more clearly the holy things they signify and that the Christian people, as far as possible, are able to understand them with ease and to take part in the rites fully, actively and as benefits a community' (*ibid.*).

Unsurprisingly the final promulgated version of the Constitution does not specifically mention the orientation of the celebrant at the altar during the celebration of the eucharist. It does contain the following mention of the altar:

> Along with the revision of the liturgical books, as laid down in Art. 25, there is to be an early revision of the canons and ecclesiastical statutes which govern the provision of material things involved in sacred worship. These laws refer especially to the worthy and well planned construction of sacred buildings, the shape and construction of altars, the nobility, placing, and safety of the eucharistic tabernacle, the dignity and suitability of the baptistery, the proper ordering of sacred images, embellishments, and vestments. Laws which seem less suited to the reformed liturgy are to be brought into harmony with it, or else abolished; and any which are helpful are to be retained if already in use, or introduced where they are lacking (SC 28).

Looking at this passage in isolation, it is true that it *could* be interpreted as having nothing to do with the direction in which the celebrant faced while presiding at the eucharist. However, due to today's debate on orientation, one of the original authors of this passage has come out to clarify that the drafts of this passage did indeed refer to the possibility of changing the location of the altar to allow for *versus populum* celebration.[80] In preparation for Vatican II, Rinaldo Falsini had been

[80]Rinaldo Falsini, 'Celebrare Rivolti al Popolo e Pregare Rivolti al Signore: Sull'Orientamento della Preghiera' in *Rivista Liturgica* 2 (mar/apr 2008). Available on-line at: http://www.rivistaliturgica.it/upload/2008/articolo2_325.asp#

appointed as a member of the pontifical preparatory commission on the liturgy, where he had the responsibility to transcribe the minutes and keep the records of the commission. During the Council he was involved in the drafting of *SC* and after the Council was involved in the *consilium* for the implementation of the constitution on the liturgy, as well as being involved in many other aspects of the conciliar reform of the liturgy and the preparation of the Italian translations of the different liturgical books. Recently, when he heard of certain authors proposing that *versus populum* celebrations had not been discussed in the Council itself and that they found their way via a back door into the post-conciliar instruction *Inter Oecumenici*, he felt obliged to tell how this was not the case.

In fact Falsini's assertion has been backed up by the recent publication of a scholarly edition of the documentation of the preparatory commission who worked preparing the various initial drafts of the document that was to become SC from June 1960 to January 1962.[81] We can see a number of different drafts that mention the possibility of celebrating mass *versus populum* starting with the initial draft of February 1961, here it recommended that the tabernacle be removed from the main altar of the church so that mass could be celebrated *versus populum*. The later drafts of the full document recommend the placement of the main altar in '*loco intermedio inter presbyterium et plebem, id est: in medio synaxeos*.'[82]

Less than two years after *SC* was promulgated the instruction *Inter Oecumenici*, prepared by the *consilium* for the carrying out of the constitution on the sacred liturgy and issued on September 26, 1964 (while the Council itself was still in session), has a chapter on the designing of new churches and altars that includes the following instruction:

---

[81]For more information see John W O'Malley, *What Happened at Vatican II* (Harvard University Press, Cambridge, MA, 2008), 129-141.

[82]This is from the January 1962 draft as found in Angelo Lameri, *La 'Pontificia Commissio de Sacra Liturgia Praeparatoria Concilii Vaticani II': Documenti, Testi, Verbali* (CLV, Rome, 2013), 360, 825.

It is better for the main altar to be constructed away from the wall so that one can easily walk around the altar and celebrate facing the people. [Praestat ut altare maius exstruatur a pariete seiunctum, ut facile circumiri et in eo celebratio versus populum peragi possit.][83]

This was followed by the following instruction in the General Instruction of the *Roman Missal* (*GIRM*) which reads:

The altar should be built apart from the wall, in such a way that it is possible to walk around it easily and that Mass can be celebrated at it facing the people, which is desirable wherever possible. The altar should, moreover, be so placed as to be truly the centre toward which the attention of the whole congregation of the faithful naturally turns. The altar is usually fixed and is dedicated.[84]

The most recent edition of the *GIRM* has become even stronger on this point and even allows for a second altar facing the people to be added to a church so that regular mass celebrated facing the people can easily be accommodated in older historical churches:

---

[83]Sacra Congregatio Rituum, *Instructio ad exsecutionem Constitutionis de sacra Liturgia recte ordinandam 'Inter Oecumenici,'* AAS 56 (1964), 898, no. 91.

[84]There have been a number of editions of the *General Instruction of the Roman Missal*, here I quote number 299 of the current Third Edition as found in Edward Foley, Nathan Mitchell and Joanne Pierce (eds), *A Commentary on the General Instruction of the Roman Missal* (Liturgical Press, Collegeville, MN, 2007), 362. The only significant change of this paragraph from the first edition in 1969 is the addition of the words 'which is desirable wherever possible.' It should be noted that the Latin of this passage is somewhat unclear. It is nearly always understood that number 299 recommends *versus populum* celebrations, however it is technically possible to translate the last clause of the first sentence in a number of different ways, some of which recommend *versus populum,* some of which only recommend the possibility of being able to walk around the altar to incense it and, while definitely permitting *versus populum* celebrations, do not specifically recommend it. See Jonathan Day's 12 July, 2016 post on the grammar of number 299 at PrayTell http://www.praytellblog.com/index.php/2016/07/12/disambiguating-the-quod-clause-in-girm-section-299/

In building new churches, it is preferable to erect a single altar which in the gathering of the faithful will signify the one Christ and the one eucharist of the Church. In already existing churches, however, when the old altar is positioned so that it makes the people's participation difficult but cannot be moved without damage to its artistic value, another fixed altar, of artistic merit and duly dedicated, should be erected and sacred rites celebrated on it alone. In order not to distract the attention of the faithful from the new altar, the old altar should not be decorated in any special way.[85]

However it must be admitted that even though the permission to celebrate the eucharist *versus populum* was very popular, it was never obligatory. Since Vatican II it has always been permissible to celebrate the eucharist *ad orientem*. In a letter addressed to the heads of bishops' conferences, dated 25 January 1966, Cardinal Giacomo Lercaro, the president of the *Consilium*, states that regarding the renewal of altars 'prudence must be our guide.' He goes on to explain:

Above all because for a living and participated liturgy, it is not indispensable that the altar should be versus populum: in the Mass, the entire liturgy of the word is celebrated at the chair, ambo or lectern, and, therefore, facing the assembly; as to the eucharistic liturgy, loudspeaker systems make participation feasible enough. Secondly, hard thought should be given to the artistic and architectural question, this element in many places being protected by rigorous civil laws.[86]

But the adoption of the *versus populum* orientation during the eucharistic prayer has been one of the most significant elements of the liturgical renewal following Vatican II. As with the vernacular, it has

---

[85]*GIRM* 303 in *ibid.*, 364. The *GIRM* has developed in its different versions and this is a new paragraph in the Third Edition.
[86]Giacomo Lercaro, 'L'Heureux Développement' in *Notitiae* 2 (1966), 160.

been virtually universal in its adoption and this adoption, although perhaps not accompanied by enough meaningful catechesis, has been welcomed by the great majority of catholics in the pews.[87] The ability to see the priest (accompanied by the adoption of the vernacular and the use of microphones in church) has allowed them actually to see what is happening in the liturgy and to hear and understand its words.

---

[87]For some of idea of the type of catechesis provided at the time see the arguments for the architectural renewal of the altar in Charles Davis, 'The Christian Altar,' in William Lockett (ed), *The Modern Architectural Setting of the Liturgy* (SPCK, London, 1964), 13-31.

7

Criticisms of the New Practice

Despite the almost universal and immediate adoption of exclusively celebrating the eucharist *versus populum* and the rearranging of the sanctuaries in the vast majority of catholic churches, to facilitate this new style of worship, not everyone was happy with this development. Balthasar Fischer[88] and, more importantly, Joseph Jungmann,[89] two of the experts who had cooperated in the revision of the liturgy after Vatican II, both pointed out that it was still possible to celebrate the eucharist *ad orientem* and that the new permission to celebrate *versus populum* was not mandatory.

In the period immediately after the Council, Louis Bouyer provided perhaps the most influential critique of the new practice.[90] His small

---

[88]Balthasar Fischer, 'Die Grundaussagen der Liturgie-Konstitution und ihre Rezeption in fünfundzwanzig Jahren' in Hansjakob Becker, Bernd Jochen Hilberath and Ulrich Willers (eds), *Gottesdienst – Kirche – Gesellschaft. Interdisziplinäre und ökumenische Standortbestimmungen nach 25 Jahren Liturgiereform*. PiLi 5 (Verlag, St. Ottilien, 1991), 422¬23.

[89]Josef Jungmann, 'Der Neue Altar' in *Der Seelsorger* 37 (1967): 375. Later on Jungmann warns us not to make the option of mass celebrated *versus populum* into 'an absolute demand, and eventually a fashion, to which one succumbs without thinking.' Jungmann, 'Der Neue Altar' in 380. However, on a theological level Jungmann's emphasis on the role of the lay-faithful in the eucharist, as well as his enormous work implementing the renewal of the liturgy in the wake of Vatican II, gave perhaps the greatest impetus for the relocation of the altar in churches after the council. See John F. Baldovin, 'The Body of Christ in Celebration: On Eucharistic Liturgy, Theology and Pastoral Practice' in Joanne M. Pierce and Michael Downey (eds), *Source and Summit: Commemorating Josef A. Jungmann, S.J.* (Liturgical Press, Collegeville, MN, 1999), 61.

[90]While Bouyer was one of the scholars who provided much of the theological foundational work for Vatican II, in the aftermath of the Council he quickly became disenchanted with the whole project. His recently published memoirs give some insights into his state of mind. Louis Bouyer, *The Memoirs of Louis Bouyer: From Youth and Conversion to Vatican II, the Liturgical Reform, and*

book, *Liturgy and Architecture* is often cited in the current debates on the orientation of the priest at mass. While the book is not a treatise on the orientation of the celebration or on the Christian altar, it does mention the placement of the altar. To be honest, the few paragraphs that he dedicates to this topic are rather mild (in particular when compared to his style when criticizing other opinions that he disagrees with). In *Liturgy and Architecture* he maintains that the Last Supper was in all likelihood celebrated on a horseshoe-shaped table with the participants all seated on the outside with the inside free for service.[91] Bouyer may well be correct in this reconstruction. But two points must be made in this regard. First of all, we simply do not know who sat where at the Last Supper. Secondly, while it would certainly be interesting to know where Jesus sat at the Last Supper, our eucharistic celebrations today are not simple re-enactments of the Last Supper.[92]Bouyer points out that the concept of sitting around a table for a meal is a Germanic custom that became popular in Europe in the Middle Ages. Then if we follow Bouyer's logic that Jesus must have presided over the Last Supper using the typical seating plan of the day and that the early Church continued using the general custom of its own day, should we say that the typical seating plan of the first century is part of the deposit of faith or ought we to follow the custom of our own day where a typical meal has people on all sides of the table, or is the liturgy somehow more than cultural sitting customs and that we need to reflect on how to celebrate it in a way that protects the sacramental core of the eucharist but is also most suited for the faithful of the place and time to appropriate as much of the grace given in the sacrament as possible?

After. John Pepino, trans. (Angelico Press, Kettering, OH, 2015), 218-230.

[91]Louis Bouyer, *Liturgy and Architecture* (University of Notre Dame Press, Notre Dame, IN, 1967), 53-54. Famously quoted in Joseph Ratzinger, *The Spirit of the Liturgy*, trans. John Saward (Ignatius Press, San Francisco, 2000), 78. 105-6.

[92]Joseph Ratzinger, *The Feast of Faith: Approaches to a Theology of the Liturgy*. trans. Graham Harrison (Ignatius Press, San Francisco, 1986), 40-45.

There has also been a notable change in the attitude of the officials in the Roman curia in more recent years. While the official reforms promulgated in the wake of Vatican II were very popular on the parish and diocesan level, these reforms are much less popular in Rome itself.[93] This hesitancy was not directed towards *versus populum* celebrations *per se*, but against many different aspects of the reform.

---

[93]Massimo Faggioli, *True Reform: Liturgy and Ecclesiology in Sacrosanctum Concilium* (Liturgical Press, Collegeville, MN 2012), 145-159; and Piero Marini, *A Challenging Reform: Realizing the Vision of the Liturgical Renewal* (Liturgical Press, Collegeville, MN, 2007), 156-157.

8

Recent Magisterial Statements on Liturgical Orientation

After the publication of the General Instruction of the third edition of the Roman Missal in 2000[94] Cardinal Christoph Schönborn of Vienna submitted a question to the Congregation for Divine Worship as to whether GIRM 299 which states that 'the altar should be built separate from the wall, in such a way that it is possible to walk around it easily and that Mass can be celebrated at it facing the people, which is desirable wherever possible,' made undesirable *ad orientem* celebrations of the ordinary form of the Roman rite. In September 2000 the Congregation issued a response that was signed by Cardinal Jorge Arturo Medina Estévez, then Prefect of the Congregation. In this response Cardinal Medina stated that:

> In the first place, it is to be borne in mind that the word expedit does not constitute an obligation, but a suggestion that refers to the construction of the altar a pariete seiunctum (detached from the wall) and to the celebration versus populum (towards the people). The clause *ubi possibile sit* (where it is possible) refers to different elements, as, for example, the topography of the place, the availability of space, the artistic value of the existing altar, the sensibility of the people participating in the celebrations in a particular church,

---

[94]The *GIRM* was published a couple of years before the Missal itself which was published in 2002.

etc. It reaffirms that the position towards the assembly seems more convenient inasmuch as it makes communication easier (cf. the editorial in Notitiae 29 [1993] 245-49), without excluding, however, the other possibility.

However, whatever may be the position of the celebrating priest, it is clear that the eucharistic sacrifice is offered to the one and triune God and that the principal, eternal, and high priest is Jesus Christ, who acts through the ministry of the priest who visibly presides as His instrument. The liturgical assembly participates in the celebration in virtue of the common priesthood of the faithful which requires the ministry of the ordained priest to be exercised in the eucharistic synaxis. The physical position, especially with respect to the communication among the various members of the assembly, must be distinguished from the interior spiritual orientation of all. It would be a grave error to imagine that the principal orientation of the sacrificial action is towards the community. If the priest celebrates versus populum, which is legitimate and often advisable, his spiritual attitude ought always to be versus Deum per Iesum Christum (towards God through Jesus Christ), as representative of the entire Church. The Church as well, which takes concrete form in the assembly which participates, is entirely turned versus Deum (towards God) as its first spiritual movement.[95]

This response clearly supports the principle that *versus populum* is indeed 'legitimate and often advisable.' On the other hand, it does not rule out the fact that there are times when the assembly is better served by celebrating in an *ad orientem* orientation.

In 2004, Pope Francis appointed Cardinal Robert Sarah as prefect of the Congregation for Divine Worship. In his role as prefect he has

---

[95]Congregatio de Cultu Divino, 'Responsa ad quaestiones de nova Institutione Generali Missalis Romani' in *CCCIC* 32 (2000): 171-72.

not published any new documents on liturgical orientation. However, on at least three occasions he has spoken in favour of a widespread readopting of the practice of an *ad orientem* orientation in regular parish celebrations. In a 2015 article in *L'Osservatore Romano* he said that 'it is entirely fitting—for everyone, priest and congregation, to turn together to the East during the penitential rite, the singing of the *Gloria*, the orations, and the eucharistic prayer.'[96] In May 2016 he renewed his call in an interview with the French magazine Famille Chrétienne.[97]

In July 2016 he issued a still more explicit call to priests to adopt an *ad orientem* orientation at the *Sacra Liturgia* Conference in London. *Sacra Liturgia* organized liturgical conferences on the conservative end of the catholic spectrum.[98] Here Cardinal Sarah proposed:

> I want to make an appeal to all priests … I believe that it is very important that we return as soon as possible to a common orientation, of priests and the faithful turned together in the same direction— Eastwards or at least towards the apse—to the Lord who comes, in those parts of the liturgical rites when we are addressing God. This practice is permitted by current liturgical legislation. It is perfectly legitimate in the modern rite. Indeed, I think it is a very important step in ensuring that in our celebrations the Lord is truly at the centre.
>
> And so, dear fathers, I ask you to implement this practice wherever possible, with prudence and with the necessary catechesis, certainly, but also with a pastor's confidence that this is something good for the Church, something good for our people. Your own pastoral

---

[96]Robert Sarah, 'Silenziosa azione del cuore' in *L'Osservatore Romano* (Italian edition, 12 June 2015, page 6). English translation from http://www.ccwatershed.org/blog/2015/aug/12/cardinal-robert-sarah-liturgical-english/

[97]http://www.famillechretienne.fr/vie-chretienne/liturgie/cardinal-sarah-comment-remettre-dieu-au-caeur-de-la-liturgie-194987#.V0bFpURrE2U.twitter

[98]To understand their liturgical philosophy, see Alcuin Reid, 'Editor's Preface' in Alcuin Reid, (ed.), *Sacred Liturgy: The Source and Summit of the Life and Mission of the Church* (Ignatius Press, San Francisco, 2014), 7-12.

judgement will determine how and when this is possible, but perhaps beginning this on the first Sunday of Advent this year, when we attend 'the Lord who will come' and 'who will not delay' may be a very good time to do this. Dear Fathers, we should listen again to the lament of God proclaimed by the prophet Jeremiah: 'they have turned their back to me.' Let us turn again towards the Lord![99]

Cardinal Sarah is absolutely correct that current liturgical law allows priests to use an *ad orientem* orientation as they preside over the eucharist according to the current Roman Missal. However, when the Cardinal Prefect of the Congregation for the Divine Worship issued such a clarion call, it was immediately spread on the internet and in the catholic media. The nuance of the difference between a private invitation made by Cardinal Sarah as a pastor and an official instruction by the Congregation that he heads was lost on many people.

Pope Francis does not exercise a very hands-on governance of the Congregation for Divine Worship, but within a few days of Cardinal Sarah's talk the Pope summoned him. After the meeting the Press Office of the Holy See issued this clarification to Cardinal Sarah's talk:

> It would appear opportune to offer clarification in the light of information circulated in the press after a conference held in London a few days ago by Cardinal Sarah, prefect of the Congregation for Divine Worship. Cardinal Sarah has always been rightly concerned about the dignity of the celebration of Mass, so as to express appropriately the attitude of respect and adoration for the Eucharistic mystery. Some of his expressions have however been incorrectly interpreted, as if they were intended to announce new indications different to those given so far in the liturgical rules and

---

[99]Robert Sarah, 'Towards an Authentic Implementation of *Sacrosanctum Concilium*,' Delivered on 5 July 2016 in London and available in English translation at http://www.ccwatershed.org/blog/2016/jul/7/robert-cardinal-sarah-address-2015-july/

in the words of the Pope regarding celebration facing the people and the ordinary rite of the mass.

Therefore it is useful to remember that in the Institutio Generalis Missalis Romani (General Instruction of the Roman Missal), which contains the norms relating to the Eucharistic celebration and is still in full force, paragraph no. 299 states that: '*Altare extruatur a pariete seiunctum, ut facile circumiri et in eo celebratio versus populum peragi possit, quod expedit ubicumque possibile sit. Altare eum autem occupet locum , ut revera centrum sit ad quod totius congregationis fidelium attentio sponte convertatur*' ('The altar should be built separate from the wall, in such a way that it is possible to walk around it easily and that Mass can be celebrated facing the people, which is desirable wherever possible. Moreover, the altar should occupy a place where it is truly the centre toward which the attention of the whole congregation of the faithful naturally turns'.)

Pope Francis, for his part, on the occasion of his visit to the Dicastery for Divine Worship, expressly mentioned that the 'ordinary' form of the celebration of the Mass is that expressed in the Missal promulgated by Paul VI, while the 'extraordinary' form, which was permitted by Pope Benedict XVI for the purposes and in the ways explained in his Motu Proprio Summorum Pontificum, must not take the place of the 'ordinary' one.

Therefore, new liturgical directives are not expected from next Advent, as some have incorrectly inferred from some of Cardinal Sarah's words, and it is better to avoid using the expression 'reform of the reform' with reference to the liturgy, given that it may at times give rise to error.

All the above was unanimously expressed during a recent audience granted by the Pope to the same Cardinal Prefect of the Congregation for Divine Worship.[100]

---

[100]Holy See Press Office Communiqué: *Some clarifications on the celebration of Mass,*

It would be hard to interpret this clarification as being anything other than a rejection on the part of the pope of Cardinal Sarah's proposal that more parish assemblies adopt an *ad orientem* orientation in their regular eucharistic celebrations.[101]

Therefore given that both orientations are valid manners of celebration, the rest of this study will examine the theological and pastoral issues involved in this pastoral choice that faces parish assemblies.

11.07.2016 available at http://press.vatican.va/content/salastampa/it/bollettino/pubbli-co/2016/07/11/0515/01177.html

[101]Perhaps we can also get a glimpse of the thought of Pope Francis on the matter in two popular works that were published in 2016. In a letter to a child, Pope Francis comments how the mass was celebrated differently in his youth and how 'the priest faced the altar, which was next to the wall, and not the people.' Even if this is a work of popular catechetics and not liturgical theology, nonetheless it shows how Pope Francis has the same attitude as the great majority of practising catholics to *ad orientem* celebrations. See Jorge Mario Bergoglio, *L'Amore Prima del Mondo: Papa Francesco Scrive ai Bambini* (Antonio Spadaro (ed), Rizzoli, Milan, 2016), 75. N.B. this letter was not included in the English translation of the book entitled *Dear Pope Francis*. In answer to a recent question on the promotion of *ad orientem* celebrations Pope Francis asserted that 'to speak of a "reform of the reform" is an error.' See Pope Francis' interview with Antonio Spadaro in Jorge Mario Bergoglio, *Nei Tuoi Occhi è la Mia Parola: Omelie e Discorsi di Buenos Aires 1999-2013* (Rizzoli, Milan, 2016), xiv.

9

The Particular Case of Joseph Ratzinger

Given the importance of the contribution of Joseph Ratzinger to this debate, and his standing as one of the greatest theologians of the twentieth century, no treatment of the orientation of the celebrant during the eucharist can be done without making reference to him. There can be little doubt that, as a theologian, Joseph Ratzinger would think that in an ideal world a priest would celebrate the mass *ad orientem*. While by no means rejecting the liturgical renewal of Vatican II wholesale, he does not see *versus populum* celebrations as being an improvement on the pre-conciliar practice of *ad orientem* celebrations. He has mentioned this many times in his theological writings. This passage in *The Spirit of the Liturgy* is a good summary of his thought:

> It would surely be a mistake to reject all the reforms of our century wholesale. When the altar was very remote from the faithful, it was right to move it back to the people. In cathedrals this made it possible to recover the tradition of having the altar at the crossing, the meeting point of the nave and the presbyterium. It was also important clearly to distinguish the place for the Liturgy of the Word from the place for the properly Eucharistic liturgy. For the Liturgy of the Word is about speaking and responding, and so a face-to-face exchange between proclaimer and hearer does make sense. In the psalm the hearer internalizes what he has heard, takes it into himself, and transforms it into prayer, so that it becomes a response. On the other hand, a common turning to the east during the Eucharistic Prayer remains

essential. This is not a case of something accidental, but of what is essential. Looking at the priest has no importance. What matters is looking together at the Lord.[102]

In particular Ratzinger often mentions that a *versus populum* celebration of the eucharist contains 'the danger … that we can make the congregation into a closed circle that is no longer aware of the explosive Trinitarian dynamism that gives the Eucharist its greatness.'[103] Given the stature of Cardinal Ratzinger as a theologian and as prefect of the Congregation of the Doctrine of the Faith, the proposal had an impact on the liturgical debate. This impact was even more felt after his election to the papacy. Yet, writing in the preface of the volume of his *Omnia Opera* dedicated to his liturgical works, he stated his surprise that his advocacy of *ad orientem* worship generated so much response:

Unfortunately almost all of the reviews jumped on a single chapter: 'The Altar and the Direction of Liturgical Prayer.' Readers of these reviews must have concluded that the whole work dealt only with the direction in which Mass is celebrated; that it was all about trying to reintroduce Mass celebrated by the priest 'with his back to the people.' Given this distortion, I thought for a while about omitting this chapter – nine pages out of a total of two hundred – so that finally a discussion could begin about essential things in the books about which I had been and am concerned.[104]

---

[102]Joseph Ratzinger, *The Spirit of the Liturgy* (trans John Saward, Ignatius Press, San Francisco, 2000), 81.

[103]Ratzinger, *Theology of the Liturgy*, 390. Ratzinger's view has been strongly influenced by Klaus Gamber. For Gamber's view see Klaus Gamber, *The Reform of the Roman Liturgy: Its Problems and Background* (Una Voce Press, San Juan Capistrano, CA, 1983), 77-89. I would recommend comparing Gamber's historical overview of liturgical orientation with my own, although I agree with his conclusion that the church adopted *versus populum* in her celebrations based on 'theological considerations,' and that the future will show whether or not this was a good decision (see *ibid.*, 89).

[104]Pope Benedict XVI, 'On the Inaugural Volume of My Collected Works' in Ratzinger, *Theology*

Yet this opinion of Cardinal Ratzinger did generate a response. His proposals were not an afterthought, they formed part of his overall vision for the renewal of the liturgy. He wrote the book with the aim of encouraging a new 'liturgical movement.'[105] So it should not be surprising that his proposal was taken up by many people.[106] In the years since *The Spirit of the Liturgy* has been published, undoubtedly to some degree inspired by Cardinal Ratzinger a number of parishes have readopted *ad orientem* worship, even if this still constitutes a tiny minority of catholic parishes world-wide.

However, whatever his views as a theologian, as Pope Benedict XVI he did not use the petrine office to promote *ad orientem* worship.[107] To the best of my knowledge during his time as pope he only celebrated one public mass a year *ad orientem* – the annual mass in the Sistine Chapel for the Baptism of the Lord (and the argument could be made that he did this because of the historic and artistic lay-out of this chapel). Another significant element in this debate is the example Pope Benedict XVI gave when the Altar of the Chair at St Peter's Basilica was replaced in 2008. This was the main renovation of a Roman Basilica during his pontificate

---

of the Liturgy, xvi.

[105]Joseph Ratzinger, *The Spirit of the Liturgy*, (trans John Saward, Ignatius Press, San Francisco, 2000), 8–9.

[106]Cardinal Ratzinger wrote a foreword to one particular book advocating a return to *ad orientem* worship. This could easily be interpreted as him giving encouragement to this suggestion. See Lang, *Turning Towards the Lord*, 9-12. This preface was also judged significant enough to be included in the volume of his collected works dedicated to his liturgical writings. See Ratzinger, *Theology of the Liturgy*, 393-395 (n.b. the title *Collected Works* is somewhat confusing, as the series will not contain all of Cardinal Ratzinger's writings but only a selection of the most significant works he has written).

[107]Pope Benedict XVI did not feel inhibited in making modifications to the liturgy. He added new dismissals to the end of mass and an invocation of St Joseph in the Second, Third and Fourth Eucharistic Prayers, and modified the prayer welcoming the child into the church in the *Rite of Infant Baptism*. Moreover, he rehabilitated the Tridentine liturgical books with the *moto proprio* entitled *Summorum Pontificum* and set the groundwork for a radical adaptation of the Roman Missal in the apostolic constitution *Anglicanorum Coetibus*.

and the new altar was made in such a way that it could be used for either *versus populum* or for *ad orientem* celebration.[108] So here there was no imposition of a preference for *ad orientem* celebration.

One custom that was adopted in many papal masses celebrated by Pope Benedict XVI was the practice of having a large crucifix in the centre of the altar. As Cardinal Ratzinger did not think that it 'would it be right, after the upheavals of past years, to press for further external changes' and promote *ad orientem* worship,[109] he promoted what has come to be referred to as the 'Benedictine' altar arrangement. This arrangement places the altar cross in the centre of the altar and up to seven candles in a line in the front of the altar, more often than not using large crosses and candles, to set up a sort of modern-day rood screen or 'open "iconostasis"'[110] between the celebrant and the people. Again this is a liturgical use proposed as a via media between *ad orientem* and *versus populum* celebration in *The Spirit of the Liturgy*:

> Moving the altar cross to the side to give an uninterrupted view of the priest is something I regard as one of the truly absurd phenomena of recent decades. Is the cross disruptive during Mass? Is the priest more important than the Lord? This mistake should be corrected as quickly as possible; it can be done without further rebuilding. The Lord is the point of reference. He is the rising sun of history. That is why there could be a cross of the Passion, which represents the suffering Lord who for us let his side be pierced, from which flowed blood and water (Eucharist and Baptism), as well as a cross of triumph, which expresses the idea of the Second Coming and guides our eyes toward it. For it is always the one Lord: Christ yesterday, today, and forever.[111]

---

[108]http://wdtprs.com/blog/2008/11/the-revolution-continues-in-st-peters-hideous-alien-altar-replaced/

[109]Joseph Ratzinger, *Theology of the Liturgy*, 388. The original essay was published in 1981.

[110]Ratzinger, *Theology of the Liturgy*, 389. The idea of a cross on the altar is a medieval development and was unknown in the early church, see Heid, 'The Altar as Centre of Prayer and Priesthood in the Early Church,' 39.

[111]Ratzinger, *The Spirit of the Liturgy*, 84.

Milwaukee, Life/Style, Sports, Business News THE MILWAUKEE JOU
• • • • Tuesday, March 6, 1984 • • • •

—Photo by James D. Pearson

Father Edward Hussli dressed as a clown to celebrate mass last month with children at St. Agnes Catholic Church

Mass by a 'clown' brings complaints

Figure Five: Milwaukee Journal Constitutional March 6, 1984[112]

---

[112]This 'Clown Mass' celebrated by Fr. Edward Hussli, associate pastor of St Agnes Milwaukee, to mark catholic schools week on 3 February 1984, is a good example of the self-referential style of liturgy that has scandalized many people. Image courtesy of the *Milwaukee Journal*.

10

Suggestions for the Best Pastoral Practice Today

It is easy to look at the past through rose-coloured glasses. The pre-conciliar church had many positive aspects, and the criticism that today's liturgies often lack reverence and that they are sometimes self-referential celebrations that do not leave enough room for the divine must be admitted.[113] However the church of the 1950s was far from perfect. Additionally that world is long gone and simply cannot be resurrected. If I compare the recollections of the Cambridge historian Eamon Duffy who reflects on the 1950's catholicism of his childhood in Dundalk, Co. Louth, Ireland, with my own present-day experience in one of the churches of Dundalk that he attended in his youth and writes about and where I recently witnessed an attempted murder during a funeral mass I was attempting to celebrate, I can only admit that the alien world that he describes has very little in common with its present-day successor; I do not think that any priest ministering in that area in the 1950s was offered a bullet-proof vest by the police to complete the grave-side services.[114] Whatever aspect of liturgy (other than those that belong to the deposit of faith) that we look at, we must admit that which was good for the

---

[113]John Baldovin, *Reforming the Liturgy: A Response to the Critics* (Liturgical Press, Collegeville, MN, 2008) is a positive contribution in this regard.

[114]Eamon Duffy, *Faith of our Fathers: Reflections on Catholic Tradition* (Continuum, London, 2004), 11-19. For my own experience in the same town see http://www.independent.ie/irish-news/gang-storms-funeral-mass-wielding-slash-hooks-and-hatchets-29771148.html

building up of the body of Christ in 1950 might not be the best practice today.

As Cardinal Ratzinger puts it 'every age must discover and express the essence of the liturgy anew.'[115] Our study of the history of the liturgy is merely informative and not normative; liturgy cannot be an archaeological recreation of some purported golden age of Christianity past.[116] The church's discernment as to the best way to celebrate today must realize that 'the liturgy is made up of immutable elements divinely instituted, and of elements subject to change. These not only may but ought to be changed with the passage of time if they have suffered from the intrusion of anything out of harmony with the inner nature of the liturgy or have become unsuited to it' (*SC* 21). It can be of great interest to us how the eucharist was celebrated in ages past, and every disciple of Christ should be interested in knowing as much as possible about the Last Supper and how the apostles celebrated the first eucharists. However, apart from the fact that we simply know so little about the specific details of the liturgical practices of the earliest church, the duty of the church today is not simply to recreate the past. The second Vatican Council had a different goal and taught that 'in the reform and promotion of the liturgy, the full and active participation by all the people is the aim to be considered before all else' (*SC* 14).

In the liturgy the priest does not act on behalf of the liturgical assembly. The ecclesiological renewal of the twentieth century highlighted the role of all the baptized as the whole Christ. In *Mediator Dei* Pope Pius XII affirmed that: 'The sacred liturgy is, consequently, the public worship which our Redeemer as Head of the Church renders to the Father, as well as the worship which the community of the faithful renders to its Founder, and through Him to the heavenly Father. It is, in short, the

---

[115]Joseph Ratzinger, *The Spirit of the Liturgy* (trans John Saward , Ignatius Press, San Francisco, 2000), 81.

[116]See Robert Taft, 'Response to the Berakah Award: Anamnesis' in *Between East and West: Problems in Liturgical Understanding* (2nd edn Pontificio Instituto Orientale Press, Rome, 1997), 289.

worship rendered by the Mystical Body of Christ in the entirety of its Head and members.'[117] Furthermore, when the eucharist is celebrated correctly 'it is no longer the Church offering Christ, but Christ is offering his Church, when, that is, the sacrifice of the Head follows that of the members.'[118]

Cardinal Ratzinger and other theologians are very right when they point out that contemporary liturgy has the danger of becoming a closed circle with little reference to the transcendental, divine aspect of the liturgy. Any honest observer must admit that there have been appalling examples of liturgical renewal in the last few decades.[119] There has been a particular tendency among some priests to become a type of media personality by placing themselves at the centre of the liturgical celebration.[120] *Versus populum* celebrations can run the risk of allowing the priest to become a sort of 'talking torso.'[121]

Some contemporary movements within catholicism favour *ad orientem* celebrations. The Society of St Peter and some newer religious orders favour the use of the extraordinary form of the Roman rite, and their liturgies are, almost without exception, celebrated *ad orientem*. Some groups prefer the so-called 'Reform of the Reform' and advocate

---

[117]*Mediator Dei 20*, Vatican translation. This is developed by Congar in his essay 'The Ecclesia or Christian Community as a Whole Celebrates the Liturgy' in Yves Congar, *At the Heart of Christian Worship: Liturgical Essays of Yves Congar* (Paul Philibert (ed and trans), Liturgical Press, Collegeville, MN, 2010), 15- 67.

[118]Henri de Lubac, *Catholicism: Christ and the Common Destiny of Man* (trans Lancelot C. Sheppard and Elizabeth England, Ignatius Press, San Francisco, 1988), 108.

[119]Baldovin, *Reforming the Liturgy*, 112. While I in no way agree with the rejection that the Society of St Pius X has of mainstream Catholicism, I can sympathize with the pain evident in the many examples of poor liturgy given in Michael Davies, *Pope Paul's New Mass* (Angelus Press, Kansas City, MO, 1980). Related to our study in this article is the physical form and artistic value of many contemporary altars. Many photographs of altars in present-day European churches are given in Boselli, *L'Altare*, however, in my opinion, some of these are not of the best artistic design and often clash with the historic churches in which they are located.

[120]Paul C. Vitz and Daniel C. Vitz, 'Messing with the Mass: The problem of Priestly Narcissism Today' in *Homiletic & Pastoral Review* (2007), 16-22.

[121]Peter J. Elliott, 'Ars Celebrandi in the Sacred Liturgy' in Alcuin Reid (ed), *Sacred Liturgy: The Source and Summit of the Life and Mission of the Church* (Ignatius Press, San Francisco, 2014), 75.

a very Baroque style of the ordinary form of the Roman rite, including liturgies that are usually celebrated *ad orientem*.[122] These intentional liturgical assemblies are an asset to the church, but they are not the church in her entirety. It must be accepted likewise that as long as the various groups have stable congregations of suitably formed members of the faithful, their celebrations can be great moments of grace for their participants. However the fact that certain currents in these movements exhibit a tendency to identify all of the church's woes today with the second Vatican Council is problematic.[123] Indeed to believe this is to be 'on the cusp of heresy' as it implies that 'the Council was not under the guidance of the Holy Spirit.'[124]

Given that these intentional communities, find spiritual benefit in the extraordinary form of liturgies inspired by it, the fundamental question is whether these liturgies should be seen as an accommodation for a particular sub-set of the faithful or as a success story that all other parish liturgies ought to aspire to. Personally, I believe that these liturgies are fundamentally a concession. A city or an extended area, such as a diocese, might be able to support one congregation celebrating in the extraordinary form, to provide a beautiful church, vestments, etc. and, more importantly, develop a schola that can sing the propers of the mass in Gregorian chant. It is also quite difficult to train priests to celebrate the intricacies of the extraordinary form.[125] Realistically, I do not believe

---

[122]See, for example, Marc Aillet, *The Old Mass and the New: Explaining the Motu Proprio Summorum Pontificum of Pope Benedict XVI* (Ignatius Press, San Francisco, 2010), 29-73; and Thomas Kocik, *Reform of the Reform? A Liturgical Debate* (Ignatius Press, San Francisco, 2003).

[123]In a recent blog post Anthony Esolen, professor of English at Providence College and a respected author on the catholic 'right', likens the celebration of the eucharist *versus populum* to shooting oneself in the foot with a shotgun, and says that this liturgical change is one of the main reasons that the catholic church is 'missing more than 300,000 priests who otherwise might have been ministering to the people of God today.' See https://www.lifesitenews.com/blogs/the-catholic-churchs-priest-shortage-crisis-a-self-inflicted-wound

[124]Richard John Neuhaus, *Catholic Matters: Confusion, Controversy, and the Splendor of Truth* (Basic Books, New York, 2006), 140.

[125]In his recently-published memoirs Bouyer tells how Fr. Joseph Jungmann, probably the greatest

that this could or should be done in every parish for every mass. It is also historically inaccurate to think that the liturgies of the 1950s formed some sort of catholic liturgical perfection. There were plenty of poor-quality liturgies before the Council.[126]

Today the vast majority of catholics have fully accepted the liturgical renewal that followed Vatican II. Indeed most catholics alive today, have been born over the last fifty years and have no memory of the pre-conciliar liturgy.[127] Even in the immediate aftermath of the Council, most catholics (and these were people who had experienced the pre-conciliar liturgy) were happy with the renewed liturgy. In one study, five years after the closing of the council, 'between 85 and 87 per cent of practising catholics in the United States said that they preferred the new Mass to that celebrated according to the sixteenth-century *Missale Romanum*.'[128] But it was not only lay people who liked the liturgical renewal. The bishops who participated in the 1985 Extraordinary Synod had been formed in seminaries prior to the Council and were intimately familiar with *ad orientem* celebration of the eucharist. Yet, when called by Pope John Paul II to reflect on Vatican II on its twentieth anniversary, they had this to say about liturgical renewal in their final report: 'The liturgical renewal is the most visible fruit of the whole conciliar effort. Even if there have been some difficulties, it has generally been received joyfully and fruitfully by the faithful.'[129]

---

scholar of the Roman rite in the twentieth century, had never actually presided at a solemn mass. If the world's expert had never celebrated a solemn mass during the pre-conciliar period, one can only imagine how difficult it would be to find a priest today who would be suitably prepared. See Bouyer, *The Memoirs of Louis Bouyer*, 221.

[126] For some examples of poor liturgical practices before the renewal of the liturgy, see Bernard Botte, *From Silence to Participation: An Insider's View of Liturgical Reform*, (trans John Sullivan , The Pastoral Press, Washington, D.C., 1988), 1-8.

[127] This is not to say that some younger catholics may have manufactured idealized 'memories' of a liturgical past they never actually experienced. See Vincent J. Miller, *Consuming Religion: Christian Faith and Practice in a Consumer Culture* (Continuum, New York, 2005).

[128] Mark S. Massa, *The American Catholic Revolution: How the Sixties Changed the Church Forever* (Oxford University Press, New York, 2010), 15.

[129] The Final Report of the 1985 Extraordinary Synod available at https://www.ewtn.com/library/CURIA/SYNFINAL.HTM

In general most people agreed that, when taken as a whole, the reform of the liturgy was a positive development in the spiritual lives of catholics. In the wake of Vatican II a more human form of worship became widespread. In this context Fergus Kerr has commented:

> The eucharistic rite in Catholic worship used to be notorious for the impersonality of its style. It is face and voice that reveal personality. The face of the celebrant remained averted throughout the greater part of the ceremony and his voice was either reduced to an anonymous murmur or distorted out of all recognition in a highpitched exotic semi-oriental chant. Now, however, the personal approach of the celebrant seems to count for a good deal in establishing the atmosphere in which the ceremony may be enjoyed.[130]

Another aspect of today's culture that pastors of souls must consider when deciding whether to celebrate *versus populum*, is the great tendency to individualize the practice of religion. Christianity cannot be simply about 'me and God,' God did not call individuals, he formed a church, an assembly of those redeemed by Christ.[131] Indeed individualism is a particular curse and danger in our modern society.[132] We come to the

---

[130]Fergus Kerr, 'Liturgy and Impersonality' in *New Blackfriars* 52 (1971), 437. However perhaps Kerr's very valid concern could benefit by being balanced by a renewed appreciation of the eschatological dimension in the eucharist. For an example of such concern (albeit heavily influenced by Ratzinger) see Albert Gerhards, '*Versus Orientem – versus populum: Zum gegenwärtigen Diskussionsstand einer alten Streitfrage*' in *Theologische Revue* 98 (2002), 15-22.

[131]On this fundamental principle of Christian liturgy see A.G. Martimort (ed), *The Church at Prayer Vol I: Principles of the Liturgy* (Liturgical Press, Collegeville, 1987), 89-111; and *Catechism of the Catholic Church*, numbers 1140-1144.

[132]See Dennis C. Smolarski, *Eucharist and American Culture: Liturgy, Unity, and Individualism* (Paulist Press, Mahwah, NJ, 2010). Pope John Paul II warned the Canadian bishops that 'the anonymity of the city cannot be allowed to enter our eucharistic communities. New ways must be found to build bridges between people, so there is that experience of mutual acceptance and closeness which Christian fellowship requires' (Address of John Paul II to the Bishops of Ontario, Canada, on their '*Ad Limina*' Visit, 4 May 1999, available at http://w2.vatican.va/content/john-paul-ii/en/speeches/1999/may/documents/hf_jp-ii_spe_19990504_ad-limina-canada-ontario.html).

eucharist to be in communion with God. St John reminds us in his first letter that 'those who say, "I love God," and hate their brothers or sisters, are liars; for those who do not love a brother or sister whom they have seen, cannot love God whom they have not seen' (1 John 4.20 NRSV). I am not implying that those who participate in a eucharist celebrated *ad orientem* hate their brothers and sisters, but I do note that physically having to contemplate them at mass is a help to overcoming any hatred or bitterness that at times all of us find festering in our hearts. When participating in the eucharistic liturgy I am obliged also to consider my brothers and sisters in Christ and not simply to ignore them and look only at the altar.[133] It is true that the human person is not the centre of the eucharistic celebration, but neither is he or she excluded. The *Catechism of the Catholic Church* tells us that the liturgical assembly is the main celebrant of sacramental liturgy:

> The celebrating assembly is the community of the baptized who, 'by regeneration and the anointing of the Holy Spirit, are consecrated to be a spiritual house and a holy priesthood, that through all the works of Christian men they may offer spiritual sacrifices.' This 'common priesthood' is that of Christ the sole priest, in which all his members participate: Mother Church earnestly desires that all the faithful should be led to that full, conscious, and active participation in liturgical celebrations which is demanded by the very nature of the liturgy, and to which the Christian people, 'a chosen race, a royal priesthood, a holy nation, a redeemed people,' have a right and an obligation by reason of their Baptism. (CCC 1141)

Another important aspect of this is the rediscovery of the eucharistic

---

[133]Paul Josef Cordes, *Una Participación Active: Aproximación Pastoral a la Celebración de la Eucaristía en Pequeñas Comunidades* (Grafite Ediciones, Baracaldo, 1998), 523; and John Baldovin, 'Idols and Icons: Reflections on the Current State of Liturgical Reform' in *Worship* 84 (2010), 396-397.

signs. This has been helped by the Anglican scholar, Dom Gregory Dix's *The Shape of the Liturgy*.[134] Rather than looking for some *ipsissima verba* or ancient exact words of Christ forming a eucharistic prayer in common usage by all the apostles and at the root of all the church's later euchological tradition, this theory claims that there is a common 'shape' to most early eucharistic liturgies. Following a liturgy of the word that was inherited from the Jewish synagogue, Dix proposed that there developed a universal fourfold eucharistic rite that was common to all Christians: '(1) the offertory; bread and wine are "taken" and placed on the table together. (2) The prayer; the president gives thanks to God over the bread and wine together. (3) The fraction; the bread is broken. (4) The communion; the bread and wine are distributed together.'[135]

In our considerations we continually return to the question of whether it is beneficial for Christians actually to see these eucharistic actions. Today's catholics have become accustomed to seeing and hearing what happens at the eucharistic celebration. This is something that is true in both the ordinary and the extraordinary forms of the Roman rite. In the extraordinary form, the personal hand-missals that many laypeople use at mass often include pictures of what the priest is doing to give some idea of what is happening on the altar for the assembly that cannot see it with their own eyes.[136] Are these better performed by the presider, allowing the assembly to see them, or is it better that the presider and

---

[134]Gregory Dix, *The Shape of the Liturgy* (Dacre Press, London, 1945; Reprinted with an Introduction by Simon Jones, Continuum, London, 2005). Many contemporary scholars reject Dix's insights, however I personally believe that they are still very relevant, see Neil Xavier O'Donoghue, 'The Shape of the History of the Eucharist', 71-83.

[135]Dix, *The Shape of the Liturgy*, 48.

[136]For example the new edition of a hand-missal for the laity, published by Corpus Christi Watershed contains a beautiful set of photographs of a priest as he celebrates mass. See *St. Edmund Campion Missal & Hymnal for the Traditional Latin Mass* (Corpus Christi Watershed, Los Angeles, CA, 2013). The website promoting the missal included the following selling point. 'A distinguishing feature of our book is the inclusion of … 100+ color photographs, made possible by the Priestly Fraternity of Saint Peter, to help the congregation follow the prayers and ceremonies.' http://www.ccwatershed.org/Campion/

the assembly face the same direction in a type of symbolic procession, where the priest is leading the people towards the Lord as they pray, but the assembly is not able actually to contemplate the eucharistic actions inherited from the Lord 'on the night he was betrayed.'[137]

There are many factors that can influence the decision of whether to celebrate the eucharist with the priest positioned *versus populum* or *ad orientem*. One of my favourite anecdotes in liturgical history gives a particular example of a Sunday service conducted by Bishop Whitford of Brechin in Angus, Scotland in 1637. Bishop Whitford was using a new edition of the *Book of Common Prayer* whose use in Scotland had been mandated by King Charles I and was much hated by the Scottish Kirk for its catholic tendencies. While most other ministers simply ignored the king's orders to use the book and while a few were attacked by angry congregants for their fidelity to the monarch, the good bishop of Brechin managed to conduct the full service that morning presiding over the liturgy facing his congregation with a loaded pistol in each hand![138] Obviously this is not the regular situation for today's celebrants, but it is a good example of how the particular considerations of another time and place are not necessarily those that should be given most weight today.

In a similar vein I would propose that our arguments for best practice today should not be exclusively based on archaeological evidence, which generally supports *ad orientem* worship (even if we do not know the details of how the earliest church celebrated). *SC* 59 tells us that:

> the purpose of the sacraments is to sanctify men, to build up the body of Christ, and, finally, to give worship to God; because they are signs they also instruct. They not only presuppose faith, but by words and objects they also nourish, strengthen, and express it; that is why they are called 'sacraments of faith.' They do indeed impart grace, but, in

---

[137]Jungmann, *The Early Liturgy to the Time of Gregory the Great* (The University of Notre Dame Press, Notre Dame, IN, 1959), 138.

[138]C.V. Wedgewood, *The King's Peace: 1637-1641* (Collins, London, 1955), 177–8.

addition, the very act of celebrating them most effectively disposes the faithful to receive this grace in a fruitful manner, to worship God duly, and to practise charity.

If the eucharist is a 'sign' that 'instructs' then perhaps the best way for it to instruct is if the assembly can actually see the ministerial actions of Christ that the presider is performing. In this way the reformed eucharistic liturgy, generally celebrated in the vernacular and *versus populum* is a good application of Vatican II's desire that 'both texts and rites should be drawn up so that they express more clearly the holy things which they signify' (*SC* 21). When the presider performs the symbolic actions of Jesus at the Last Supper in such a way that the faithful can contemplate the Lord's gestures, then the eucharistic celebration has correctly achieved one of its aims, namely that of nourishing, strengthening, and expressing by words and actions, the faith of the assembly entering into the paschal mystery of Christ who handed himself over to death for us (see *SC* 59).[139] Indeed the *Catechism of the Catholic Church* tells us that, 'the ordained minister is, as it were, an "icon" of Christ the priest. Since it is in the eucharist that the sacrament of the church is made fully visible, it is in his presiding at the eucharist that the bishop's ministry is most evident, as well as, in communion with him, the ministry of priests and deacons' (*CCC* 1142).[140] Additionally many examples have been given in this Study

---

[139]I am indebted to Pedro Farnés for this argument. There is an interesting dialogue on *ad orientem* worship between Farnés and Cardinal Ratzinger. Farnés wrote a review of *The Spirit of the Liturgy* for the Spanish journal *Phase* and sent it to Cardinal Ratzinger who responded in the following issue (both published in 2002 in *Phase* number 42). See my English translation of these 'The Farnés, and Ratzinger Dialogue on *The Spirit of the Liturgy*' in *Antiphon* 20.2 (2016), 75-95.

[140]However, this argument is rejected by some modern proponents of women's ordination, as they favour *ad orientem* celebrations which facilitate a theology where the eucharist is understood as a 'threshold' between God and humanity and where the priest represents both Christ and the assembly. See Sarah Coakley, '"In Persona Christi": Who, or Where, is Christ at the Altar?' in Eugene E. Lemcio (ed), *A Man of Many Parts: Essays in Honor of John Westerdale Bowker on the Occasion of his Eightieth Birthday* (Pickwick Publications, Eugene, OR, 2015), 95-112; and Sarah Coakley, 'The Woman at the Altar: Cosmological Disturbance or Gender Subversion' in *The New Asceticism:*

of the importance that people have given to seeing the eucharistic bread and being close to the altar throughout history. Eucharistic devotion is an important element of catholic spirituality. It should be no surprise that many catholics have found a deeper eucharistic faith by attending eucharistic liturgies where they have been able to see the sacramental actions of the priest who celebrated facing them, so that they can more easily participate in the celebration.

Figure Six: A *versus populum* altar that is not a 'closed circle'[141]

Another factor that I perceive today is that there are many more priests who desire *ad orientem* worship than the assemblies that they serve. Even though Pope Benedict XVI gave very liberal permission for the celebration of the extraordinary form of the Roman rite, and some new extraordinary form liturgies did come about in many places, still the

---

Sexuality, Gender and the Quest for God (Bloomsbury/ Continuum, London, 2015), 55-83. N.B. Coakley attributes her insights to Orthodox theology and, in particular, to Kallistos Ware, 'Man, Woman and the Priesthood of Christ' in Thomas Hopko (ed), *Women and the Priesthood* (2nd edn St. Vladimir's Press, Crestwood, NY 1999), 47-49.

[141]St Anthony's Chapel, Redemptoris Mater Seminary, Kearny, NJ. Photo © Joe Polillio, used with permission.

vast majority of practising catholics have continued to participate in the ordinary form, with well over 99% of eucharistic liturgies being celebrated using the Paul VI edition of the Roman missal. But some priests decide that their assemblies would be better served by celebrating *ad orientem*. The celebrant faces various legitimate options. It is theoretically possible that an assembly could be composed of people who would benefit more from an *ad orientem* celebration, but the mass does not belong to the priest and he is not permitted to impose his spirituality and personal preferences on the assembly. The GIRM gives an important instruction regarding the different elements of celebrating the eucharist:

> The pastoral effectiveness of a celebration will be greatly increased if the texts of the readings, the prayers, and the liturgical songs correspond as closely as possible to the needs, spiritual preparation, and culture of those taking part. This is achieved by appropriate use of the wide options described below.
>
> The priest, therefore, in planning the celebration of Mass, should have in mind the common spiritual good of the people of God, rather than his own inclinations. He should, moreover, remember that the selection of different parts is to be made in agreement with those who have some role in the celebration, including the faithful, in regard to the parts that more directly pertain to each.
>
> Since, indeed, a variety of options is provided for the different parts of the mass, it is necessary for the deacon, the lectors, the psalmist, the cantor, the commentator, and the choir to be completely sure before the celebration about those texts for which each is responsible is to be used and that nothing be improvised. Harmonious planning and carrying out of the rites will be of great assistance in disposing the faithful to participate in the eucharist.[142]

---

[142] *GIRM* 352 in Foley, Mitchell and Pierce (eds), *A Commentary on the General Instruction of the Roman Missal*, 406-407.

In this vein it must also be emphasized that just because the presider can be seen when he celebrated *versus populum* that this does not give him free rein to entertain the assembly. A eucharistic liturgy celebrated *versus populum* can evoke a true sense of the sacred 'but only if the celebrant has a developed *ars celebrandi*.'[143] In this sense it might be worth mentioning that Lang proposes the possibility of a 'liturgical east' whereby the celebrant can face the apse, and this is considered to be east even when the church is not built on an east-west axis.[144] Would it not be possible to bring his suggestion one step forward and consider that when a eucharist is celebrated in a dignified way both the priest and people face a 'liturgical east' even when they celebrate the eucharist facing each other across the altar on which the bread and wine are placed and prayed over? The celebrant is facing *both* the people and the liturgical east when he is celebrating the eucharist. The faithful face the celebrant, who acts *in persona Christi*, contemplate the sacramental actions of the liturgy, listen to the words of the prayers *and* also face Christ in an eschatological sense as they face 'liturgical east.' 'It is neither the facing the compass east which is important, nor the presider and people facing in the same direction, but what is vital is that the presider and the assembly face the apse together, what, however, is absolutely vital is that all who celebrate the eucharist face Christ and through their participation in the sacred mysteries proclaim the Lord's death until he comes again (see 1 Cor 11.26). In this way the eschatological dimension of the eucharist will be given its correct importance, as it is true that Christ who will come *ad orientem* at the end of time to judge the living and the dead, also comes for each and every one of us whenever the holy eucharist is celebrated.[145]

---

[143]Elliott, 'Ars Celebrandi,' 80.

[144]Lang, *Turning Towards the Lord*, 84-86.

[145]Moreton, 'Orientation as a Liturgical Principle,' 589.

JLS 83

JOINT LITURGICAL STUDIES

This Study tells how from early times the Roman Catholic mass was generally celebrated with the prie[st] facing East across the altar. The people thus saw the back view of a vested minister performing a ritual large[ly] hidden from them; and any consequent sense of the solemnity and even the secrecy of that ritual was viewed a[s] integral to the nature of the sacrament, to be honoured and preserved. The Churches of the Reformation too[k] a different view, but the Roman use sailed on undisturbed, and even reinforced, by the radical attacks of th[e] Reformers. This was the use which was imitated by the anglo-catholic movement in the Church of England i[n] the nineteenth century, and then widely adopted in Anglicanism.

However, the Study shows that in the twentieth century, within the Roman Catholic Church itsel[f] questions arose as to whether this practice was theologically necessary or pastorally helpful. Some experimen[t] preceded Vatican II; but it was in the wake of the post-conciliar liturgical reforms that changes spread acro[ss] almost the whole of the global Communion – the eucharistic president taking his position behind a free standing altar, facing westward, or, as stated here, *versus populum*. This in turn provided the people with a fu[ll] view of what he did, with implications for both his ceremonial actions and for their participation.

The story did not end there; and the Roman Catholic Church has seen a reaction led or supported b[y] some eminent leaders, including Pope Benedict XVI. Evaluating the theological principles of that reaction ha[s] provided extra colour to the Study; but the author's final words concern 'Best Pastoral Practice Today'.

The author, Neil Xavier O'Donoghue, is a priest of the Archdiocese of Newark, NJ in the USA, and [is] currently the vice-rector of the Redemptoris Mater Seminary in Dundalk in the Archdiocese of Armagh i[n] Ireland. He has written extensively on liturgical matters, including a study of St Patrick and *The Eucharist i[n] Pre-Norman Ireland*, and brings all his historical acumen and theological discernment into this new and time[ly] Study.

The Alcuin Club promotes the study of Christian Liturgy, especially of the Anglican Communion. I[t] publishes an annual Collection, and has shared with GROW since 1987 in also publishing the *Joint Liturgica[l] Studies*. Members receive all publications free. For details of membership contact: The Alcuin Club, S[t] Anne's Vicarage, 182 St Ann's Hill, London SW18 2RS. Telephone: 0208 874 2809. E-mail: gordon.jeanes@ stanneswandsworth.org.uk

The Group for Renewal of Worship (GROW) has for 50 years been a focus for forward-thinking, ofte[n] adventurous, explorations in Anglican worship. It has since 1971 produced from its own members writing, o[r] its commissioning of others, over 200 titles in the Grove Worship Series, and until 1986 also produced *Grov[e] Liturgical Studies*, before joining the Alcuin Club to provide the present Joint series. Enquiries about GROW can [be] sent to Grove Books Ltd, Ridley Hall Road, Cambridge CB3 9HU, or to members of the Group.

HYMNS ANCIENT AND MODERN
13a Hellesdon Park Road, Norwich, Norfolk NR6 5DR, UK
Telephone: 01603 785900   Fax: 01603 785915
e-mail: jls@hymnsam.co.uk
Printed in Great Britain by Hobbs, Hampshire

ISSN: 0951-2667
ISBN 978-1-84825-960-7

Alcuin Club and The Group for Renewal of Worship

9 781848 259607 >

Decoding Daniel

Reclaiming the Visions of Daniel 7–11

Ernest Lucas

GROVE

BIBLICAL

SERIES